Seven Men Who Rule the World from the Grave

Seven Men Who Rule the World from the Grave

Dave Breese

MOODY PUBLISHERS
CHICAGO

All Scripture quotations, unless noted otherwise, are from the *New Scofield Reference Bible*, King James Version. Copyright © 1967 by Oxford University Press, Inc. Reprinted by permission.

The publisher wishes to thank Georgeann Shaw, Wheaton College Library, Wheaton, Illinois, and Joe Ragont Studios, Rolling Meadows, Illinois, for research assistance in securing materials pertaining to the illustrations for this volume.

ISBN: 978-0-8024-8448-2

We hope you enjoy this book from Moody Publishers. Our goal is to provide high-quality, thought-provoking books and products that connect truth to your real needs and challenges. For more information on other books and products written and produced from a biblical perspective, go to www.moodypublishers.com or write to:

Moody Publishers
820 N. LaSalle Boulevard
Chicago, IL 60610

19 20

Printed in the United States of America

To Elmer and Emma Flaming,
who gave to me
their daughter
and their love

Contents

Preface

The Gods of the Mind

The means by which one person is able to rule many others is a fascinating subject of study. Invariably, the explanation of such control is that it is a matter of the mind. Any ruler, no matter how numerous his weapons or great his wealth, must finally rule by other means. He must rule by persuasion, the ultimate weapon through which influence on a culture is produced and sustained. The truly powerful leader must influence the minds of men.

To do this, he must produce in the minds of others something more, something stronger, something more compelling than what we normally call an idea. This "thing" he must produce within the minds of others actually exists, but in the form of a mental construct. It is an image the influencer sets up in the minds of others, an image that can become an object of occupation, then of concentration, and then—dare we say it—of veneration. The influencer must produce in the minds of those he influences a kind of little god. This god of the mind is a "real thing" he plants in the mentality of unsuspecting people. This "real thing" may externally resemble Marx, Lenin, or Freud, but in reality it is a thing unto itself. It goes beyond the limitations of ordinary personality and takes on dimensions of near deity. Possibly that is why one of the strongest prohibitions in Scripture is the statement "Thou shalt have no other gods before me."

Thou shalt have no other gods before me. When the God of the universe uttered those words, He was giving an *absolute* command that applied to all things in all places for all time, until the end of time and beyond.

Obedience to that command is the key to everything. No benefit in this or in *any* possible world comes apart from the diligent conformity to that eternal and changeless rule.

Conversely, disobedience to that inflexible order results in the irretrievable loss of everything—sanity, security, rationality, health, happiness, civility, civilization—for the rule God uttered has to do with ultimate good and the final basis of all things, with the foundation for all foundations, the measure of all measures.

Every adverse fortune of life in history for men and nations has come from ignoring that command. The degree of ill present in that adverse fortune is in direct proportion to the degree an action has deviated from that command.

In fact, there is a sense in which the command "Thou shalt have no other gods before me" is not finally a command but rather a devastating, simple statement of diamond-hard reality. It is a total absolute, nonnegotiable in the slightest aspect. It is not altered by rhetoric, softened by tears, weakened by reflection, eroded by time, cowed by resentment, or defeated by successive waves of frantic assault by legions of froth-mouthed enemies.

That command is so obviously the essence of existence one marvels that it should ever be questioned by a mind that claims rationality or by a soul that quests for life. So essential is that command to rational life, the thought or the action that directs itself otherwise should be seen by all for what it is: a perverse dementia, a strange insanity.

But alas, strange insanities exist, present in our time as in virtually all times. History is filled with accounts of other gods. Individuals, then whole families, then entire nations, then teeming civilizations allowed, respected, and finally worshiped pagan deities. We read the record, which has always astonished us, of men and women by the millions who have worshiped someone or something else beside the true and living God.

Adding to our wonder, we learn that this worship has not been mere obeisance. No, indeed, it has taken the form of expensive, poverty-producing offerings placed upon the stone knees of dumb idols. Worse, this worship has taken the form of human sacrifice, infanticide, immolation, and suicide—all for gods of wood or stone that cannot speak. Worshipers have led their tiny children, their trembling wives, even their nations into the cauldron of sacrifice for other gods.

No one knows how much of the substance of life has been poured out before the graven images of time, upon the stained altars of gods who are *not* and of demons who *are*. Yes, successive generations of pitiful human beings have sunk with hardly a shriek or a tear into Sheol while still pursuing the hope of placating a crudely sculptured stone to which they have attached the name *god*. They have fantasized that they can be nurtured from stone breasts or reenlivened from the loins of a moldering statue. The mind reels in the attempt to understand the insanity of paganism.

But the gods of stone are not the whole story. Paganism has taken many forms. In Greece the mystery religions and the muses became objects of worship. Statues of deities were few, but the gods of the mind were many.

From those gods of the mind came what we now call *philosophy*—the love of thinking, the affection for the concept of things. Philosophy, a respectable pursuit in its place, has become in our time the word for all seasons. We have a philosophy of life, a philosophy of the future—yes, even a philosophy of religion.

Now there has been added "his philosophy" and "her philosophy." Philosophy has come to mean simply a set of ideas collected from one spot and another and formed into a composite that people call *a point of view*. This point of view has itself now become sacrosanct, so that one's philosophy is revered as something to which we all "have a right."

"She has a right to her views," we are told. "His ideas are his own, and they work for him," we are informed. And thus must end all discussion, of course.

So diverse have become the basic ideas about life that the notion has emerged that there is no final idea, no absolute truth. Our generation is beset with this notion of the absence of finality. "Who is to say who is right?" is the question of dismissal in many a conversation. What's more, many who so aver can point to the fallen gods of our time as proof of the instability and non-finality of the best ideas of this world.

Indeed, many an ideology important yesterday seem idiotic in the present, to the point that people are embarrassed to have believed in them. The statue of Lenin hanging by the neck as if in execution before it finally fell into a Budapest square expresses the spirit of the age: "There are no absolutes."

But, alas, to say that there are no absolutes is to say that there is no God. And if there are no absolutes, how can one confess an absolute in the negative? The mind cannot do so, for the statement is a self-contradiction. The mind reacts, stretching out tendrils like a vine in a crannied wall, seeking the next solidity to which it may attach itself. Those questing tendrils are reaching in many directions today. Some even profess to have found that set of principles on which they can ultimately rely.

To aid in our thinking about first and second principles, we must emphasize again the divine prohibition: "Thou shalt have no other gods before me." That is the rule. There must be no other first principle other than God and His Law.

By the same standard, there must also be no other central motivation, no other final goal, no other pursuit or prize, no multiple destinations. We must be ruled by no other human or subhuman creature, alive or dead. But, alas, despite many protestations, the world of our time is put upon, influenced—yes, *ruled* by the philosophies of others. I suggest, in fact, that our generation is so conformed to the ideas that have come down to us largely from preceding decades, even the previous century and the formative years of this century, that it can be said that the modern mind is ruled by men who are now in the grave.

Men who rule the world from their graves still press their philosophies upon us. We will not presume to call them "other gods," but we cannot help noting that the degree of reverence bestowed upon them is more than natural men deserve. They are called "world changers," "seminal thinkers," "sublime conceptualists," "god intoxicated," "creators," "custodians of the future," and the like. Some indeed have gone so far as to repudiate every predecessor, begetting a "new school of thought"—yes, even "a new humanity." All seven initiated a way of thinking that has affected future generations profoundly. In a sense they fathered a new *zeitgeist*. They reached into the minds, indeed the imaginations (which is sometimes more important), of tens and then millions of questing people in their own and future generations.

Their ideas, and successive corruptions of those ideas, have been taught in our schools, promoted in the media, and preached from our pulpits to the point that they are now largely unquestioned and unrefuted, having become the conventional wisdom. Having endured this far, their ideas may even be carried as foundational elements into the next millennium. Should that be the case, the next millennium may also, as has this one, refuse to bring forth the utopia most of the seven seminal thinkers have implied and some have promised. Concerning the future, time will tell. But time is already telling this generation that it must look higher than a row of tombstones for its inspiration, its knowledge, its direction from here on out.

Remembering the deadly persistence of the gods of the mind to work upon us, we may well note the call—yes, the command, which God gives to the world. The Scripture says, "He commands all men everywhere to repent." The unfortunate English translation of *metanoia* serves to obscure its real meaning. *Metanoia* means "a change of mind." Before a person can step into true reality, he must change his mind. This is commanded to all men everywhere.

We do not do violence to truth when we suggest that God is requiring a world to depose the gods of the mind and receive within that cleansed mind the true God, the Lord of glory. When we consider how the god of this world has blinded the minds of them who believe not, lest the light of the glorious gospel of Christ who is the image of God should shine unto them, we sense the importance of the mind to God—and to the devil. Satan works daily to prevent in any person an enlightened mind. By contrast, God promises that we are transformed by the renewing of our minds. Within the mind of man is resident his great capability, which is to give assent to the truth of God and to depose and send into exile the false gods that persistently work to confuse the mind.

Acknowledgments

One finds it difficult to acknowledge properly or even to remember adequately all the people, the influences, and the inspirations that produced the thoughts and the conclusions this author has deemed so valuable. Since seminary days many years ago, I have considered with some intensity why the world is what it is. These thoughts have gradually coalesced around the names of seven men who are so often noted in secular literature.

This, then, gives me the opportunity to thank the marvelous faculty of Northern Baptist Seminary, who initially engendered within my mind these ideas. Those were the days of Charles W. Koller, Carl F. H. Henry, Harold Lindsell, C. Adrian Heaton, Arnold Schultz, Julius Mantey, Faris D. Whitesell, and the blessed Maude Groom, the Greek language's finest friend. These dear and scholarly people I thank most deeply. They labored better than they knew.

Personal association with many of the places where these seven influential men lived has been a privilege indeed. London, Rome, Berlin, Paris, Amsterdam, Brussels, and a score of villages have been in my travels. I have visited the grave of Darwin in Westminster Abbey, of Marx in Highgate Cemetery, and other noted places. These travels were often in connection with the early conquests and crusades of the Youth For Christ movement. To Torrey Johnson, Bob Cook, Ted Engstrom, and others of those early stimulators of global activity I am grateful.

My special thanks to my dear Carol, who listened and communicated in a thousand conversations concerning these things. She, along with our Christian Destiny staff, made possible my related endeavors during which these pages came together.

Finally my thanks to a very talented young man: John Klaassen. He labored valiantly over the word processor, typing the manuscript and not losing the footnotes. In the process (but not because of it), he became my son-in-law. God bless him and Noelle.

And God bless you.

Introduction

"There is a tide in the affairs of men."

Truer words were, in all probability, never spoken by Shakespeare or any other who looked at the turning pages of history and their influence upon our lives. The certainty is that men and nations have not infrequently been caught in the swirling tide of multiple events, which tide takes to itself a life of its own. In fact, there have been eras in the history of our beleaguered world in which multiple sets of tide-like influences have impacted upon a civilization and its culture at nearly the same time. It has therefore become popular for commentators to speak about such things as "a crossroads of history" and similar expressions that would suggest that we are at a confluence of historic tides.

Such a time and such a confluence has been the twentieth century. It is called by some "this fabulous century," and such a denotation is not without reason. In a relatively short span of time within this century, the world has experienced many remarkable changes in the realms of science, technology, medicine, space, and a hundred other well-known ways of describing "modern times." Strangely, this century has also seen more developments that would come under the column "distressing things" than any previous century: devastating wars and monstrous new weapons. The new biological, nuclear, and chemical means mankind has of exterminating itself are a wonder to all.

Awesome is at least the word for it. Better words might well be *provocative, challenging, dangerous,* and even *adventurous.* At least we must all agree that our generation lives in the midst of a swirling tide of events, dreams, promises, threats, and changing ideas of the present and the future. Certainly our century has been the most politically interesting, the bloodiest, the most revolutionary, and the most unpredictable of any century in history. This confluence of strange conditions presses this generation to ask and answer anew such questions as, Why am I here? What is the purpose of life? and especially, Why is life and reality the way it is?

The question, Why are things the way they are? has been asked by successive generations of curious men from the dawn of history until this very moment.

The question is not a superficial intellectual exercise. No, indeed, for what we view as determining the nature of life in this world and what our response is to that nature is the cornerstone of our living. It is a truism that a person can be expected to put into practice tomorrow what he believes today. That is true of individuals, groups, nations, and entire cultures. Again and again it must be asserted that to believe in the wrong engine of history or the wrong purpose of living can lead to grievous errors, great tragedies, and devastating consequences. Conversely, to have a correct view of man, God, and history is the key to sanity and survival for individual men and for the entire culture.

In this century our culture has experienced many dark and fateful events. The leaders of our time are bewildered when they are called upon to explain the reasons that our world is the way it is or to suggest a direction for the future. Many in positions of public trust confess that they are just trying to keep the lid on, and others have abandoned even that hope.

The contradictions of the present and of what we can see of the future are overwhelming to many. That is so because few persons today have taken the time to evaluate the issues and agree with the true and resist the false. Many believe that they are borne along by streams of intellectual and philosophical influence that are of their own choosing—but alas, they have not chosen at all. Rather, a high percentage of men and nations today are ruled by a few, select seminal thinkers who, though they are now in their graves, still have influence through their ideas, convictions, and obsessions. Much of modern education, commercial interaction, social planning, intellectual conviction, and even religion is still guided by the constructs formulated by those thinkers of an earlier generation.

Everyone agrees that there is something profoundly wrong with our world. In that wrong actions and wrong results spring from wrong premises, we would do well to consider the assumptions that govern our society. As we try to articulate those assumptions, we may find ourselves standing before grave markers silently asking, *Why did you think the way you did? Why did you say what you said to us?* We can find the answers to those questions in the pages written by the men before whose graves we stand and in the words they spoke to others. It is my hope that by remembering what was believed and preached by seven men who rule the world from the grave the reader will come to know himself better and be better able to understand his generation.

I also hope that out of this understanding a vast, societal-wide change of mind may take place in which men are transformed by the renewing of their minds and the world is reoriented toward a better destiny than the fate toward which it now stumbles.

Yes, even at this late hour we may yet open the windows of our minds to a clearer, stronger voice, a voice emanating from a higher provenance than the graves of those who are now gone but whose influence still remains. We may well profit by hearing from the seven men who rule the world from their graves. If we do not, we may find ourselves occupying the eighth grave at Esdraelon, the grave of humanity itself.

I am aware of the reactions that will inevitably come from those who study these pages. The first reaction will certainly be in the form of a question: *Why did you not include Mr. So-and-so?* I assure my readers that I have a real interest in the views and careers of a hundred other characters in history who started influential movements and, more important, were the source of seminal ideas. Having taught philosophy in days gone by, I have studied with interest the ideas of many and have evaluated with appreciation the accomplishments of some and with loathing the activities of others. This having been said, I believe that the seven men discussed in this volume were the progenitors of the most influential movements of this century. Each man was himself influenced by others, but each forged some new concept that became tidal and global. Each man presented his views in so piercing, strident, fanatical, and forceful a way as to produce a social penetration. For each of them, *believing* a view was not enough. You had to act on it. And that they did, driving their ideas like spears into the social structure of their time. Those spears have not been removed to this day.

I am aware that I will be accused of reductionism in this discussion. I confess myself to be guilty as charged. Most of the men presented here have had multiple biographers, and some have had literally hundreds of texts written about them, their lives, their views, and their continuing influence. More than two hundred biographies have been written about Napoleon Bonaparte, the dictator who once ruled more of Europe than any other, and yet he is not one of the seven seminal thinkers discussed in this volume. That is because the men of whom we speak in this book ruled the world more permanently than did the fleeting human rocket that was Napoleon. The seven in this book ruled the world more permanently because they and their ideas became gods of the mind rather than masters of real estate. For them, the battle for the minds of men was the ultimate thing.

It is impossible to say in a chapter or two all that could be said about such thinkers, men of whom whole books have been the subject. I have instead dealt with the particular aspect of their thinking that penetrated the culture. Other considerations regarding their lives, their loves, and their travels, although not uninteresting, would call for further, later consideration. This book, however, will deal primarily with the way in which the seven have contended for our minds.

1

Biology Is Destiny:
Charles Darwin

"After having been twice driven back by heavy southwestern gales, Her Majesty's ship *Beagle*, a ten-gun brig, under the command of Fitzroy, RN, sailed from Devonport on the twenty-seventh of December, 1831. . . .

"The object of the expedition was to complete the survey of Patheonia and Tierra del Fuego, commenced under Captain King in 1826 to 1830—to survey the shores of Chile, Peru, and of some islands in the Pacific—and to carry a chain of chrono-metrical measurements round the World. On the sixth of January, we reached Teneriffe, but were prevented landing by fears of our bringing the cholera; the next morning we saw the sun rise behind the rugged outline of the Grand Canary island, and suddenly illumine the peak of Teneriffe, whilst the lower parts were veiled in fleecy clouds. This was the first of many delightful days never to be forgotten. On the sixteenth of January, 1832, we anchored at Porto Praya, in St. Jago, the chief island of the Cape de Verde archipelago."[1]

---

1. Charles Darwin, *The Voyage of the Beagle* (New York: New American Library, 1972; first published in 1839; known also as *Journal of Researches into the Geology and Natural History of the Various Countries Visited by H.M.S. Beagle, 1832-36*), p. 1.

Those are the opening words of a diary. Similar entries have been made in similar diaries in the early days of many a voyage from many a port down through history across the world. This entry, however, is something special. It is the beginning of a diary that was to become one of the most important in history, a diary that would chronicle a set of experiences that led to a decisive shift in thinking about the natural sciences, a change that would, in turn, influence the world of thought outside the natural sciences, leading ultimately to changes in the entire culture of many a nation.

So it was that in the introduction to a 1972 reprinting of the diary Walter Sullivan said:

> This book was prelude to what became probably the most revolutionary change that has ever occurred in man's view of himself. The change, in fact, has still not fully run its course. It demands that we regard ourselves as inseparably a part of nature and accept the fact that our descent was from more primitive creatures and, ultimately, from the common origin of all life on earth. It is the view that we will never fully understand ourselves until we understand our origins and the traits—chemical, biological, and behavioral—that we share with other species.[2]

Those are large, ambitious words, but Sullivan is accurate in saying that the diary led to "the most revolutionary change that has ever occurred in man's view of himself," for the adventure that was so significant and informative for the writer that it grew into a set of concepts, then a book, and then an approach to life, was to change fundamentally man's very understanding of himself.

The writer of the diary was Charles Darwin.

The diary was *The Voyage of the Beagle*, Darwin's account of the expedition that embraced the five most exciting years of his life. In fact, most of what occurred in his life before the voyage Darwin held to be but the prelude to the expedition to the shores of South America, and most of what came afterward was meditative and sedentary, a life characterized by illness and reclusion, but mostly by the recounting of the observations of the *Beagle* voyage. It was as if Darwin lived on those memories.

2. Ibid., p. vii.

What Darwin formulated came to be seen as a plausible new understanding of man and nature important enough to be thought the work of a genius and the beginning of a new epoch in world history. In the years following the publication of the diary (1836) and the books that grew out of the experiences described in the diary, most notably the landmark *On the Origin of Species by Means of Natural Selection* (1859), the academic world has attempted to repudiate its pre-Darwinist past and to think of mankind as part of a common continuum with nature and the universe. This intellectual revolution has caused man to reinterpret his past, rethink his present, and revise his anticipations for the future. Darwin is seen as giving the world a comprehension of itself so unlike the view held in the past that, in a sense, he restarted history. Darwin's influence continues to be pervasive today, and he holds a leading rank among those men who rule the world from the grave.

Who was this man, and what was the intellectual revolution he produced?

Charles Robert Darwin was born in 1809 to a family already given to a tradition of involvement in the world of thought as it intersected the world of biology and botany. Darwin's grandfather was the well-known Erasmus Darwin (1731-1802), a physician and man of letters, known especially for his poetry. Erasmus Darwin practiced medicine as a physician in Lichfield, England, and cultivated a botanical garden. He was the author of a long poem, *The Botanic Garden*, written in 1789, in which he expanded the botanical system of the earlier botanist Linnaeus. In another work, *Zoonomia*, Erasmus Darwin attempted to explain organic life along the lines of evolutionary principles, a presentation that anticipated Charles's later theories.

Young Darwin's educational career was somewhat inconclusive. He studied medicine at Edinburgh, but could not stomach surgery without anesthetics. He then changed to ministerial studies at Cambridge, though he lost interest in the ministry during those college years. Referring to that period of his life, Darwin said in his autobiography:

> From what little I had heard or thought on the subject, I had scruples about declaring my belief in all the dogmas of the church

of England; although otherwise I liked the thought of becoming a country clergyman. Accordingly, I read with care Pearson on the Creed, and a few other books on divinity, and as I did not then in the least doubt the strict and literal truth of every word in the Bible, I soon persuaded myself that our creed must be fully accepted.[3]

He observed in his autobiography: "Considering how fiercely I have been attacked by the orthodox, it seems ludicrous that I once intended to be a clergyman."[4] In later years he reacted against what he considered to be the narrowness of the orthodox literalists, who opposed him.

Darwin's interest in natural history led him in his college years to a friendship with J. S. Henslow, the well-known botanist of that day. It was through Henslow's urging and arrangements that young Darwin was invited to become the official naturalist aboard the *Beagle* for the five-year cruise. Darwin saw this as the vital period of his life in which his attentions were focused on the field that was to become the occupation of his life. On the cruise aboard the *Beagle* he gave himself to the accumulation, assimilation, codification, and intensive study of the data, work that led him to develop a theory to account for the way in which the various species came to be differentiated from one another.

That concept is now known as Darwinism.

In the introduction to *Origin of the Species*, the volume that grew out of the experiences described in the diary, Darwin recounted those days and the compelling influence they had upon his emergent young mind.

> When on board the *H.M.S. Beagle*, as naturalist, I was much struck with certain facts in the distribution of the organic beings inhabiting South America, and in the geological relations of the present to the past inhabitants of that continent. These facts, as will be seen in the later chapters of this volume, seem to throw some light on the origin of the species—the mystery of mysteries, as it has been called by one of our greatest philosophers. On my return home, it occurred to me, in 1837, that something might

3. Charles Darwin, *Charles Darwin's Autobiography* (New York: Henry Schuman, 1950), p. 26.
4. Ibid., p. 26.

perhaps be made out on this question by patiently accumulating and reflecting on all sorts of facts which could possibly have any bearing on it. After five years' work, I allowed myself to speculate on the subject, and drew up some short notes; these I enlarged in 1844 into a sketch of the conclusions, which then seemed to me probable. From that period to the present day, I have steadily pursued the same object. I hope that I may be excused for entering on these personal details, as I give them to show that I have not been hasty in coming to a decision.[5]

What were the conclusions to which Darwin came as a result of his research as naturalist on the *Beagle*?

Let it first be noted that Darwin had a touch of humility about his conclusions. "I am well aware that scarcely a single point is discussed in this volume in which facts cannot be adduced, often apparently leading to conclusions directly opposite to those at which I have arrived."[6]

The overarching conclusion, and what may well be called the index of Darwinism, is the concept he called, and we continue to call, *natural selection*. Darwin himself attempted to explain the concept:

> As many more individuals of each species are born than can possibly survive; and as, consequently, there is a frequently recurring struggle for existence, it follows that any being, if it vary however slightly in any manner profitable to itself, under the complex and sometimes varying conditions of life, it will have a better chance of surviving, and thus be *naturally selected*. From the strong principle of inheritance, any selected variety will tend to propagate its new and modified form.[7]

Thus we have Darwin's definition of the core of his evolutionary faith—the natural selection of individuals who have won the competition for scarce resources. Those individuals whose distinctive capacities gave them a better chance of survival in the surrounding environment lived, and lived long enough to pass on their particular genetic makeup to the next genera-

5. Charles Darwin, *The Origin of the Species* (New York: New American Library, 1958; first published in 1859 under the title *On the Origin of Species by Means of Natural Selection, or the Preservation of Favoured Races in the Struggle for Life*), p. 27.
6. Ibid., p. 28.
7. Ibid., p. 29.

tion. Over time these slight differences accumulated, with the result that eventually organisms emerged that no one would claim were the same species. Herbert Spencer was later to coin the phrase "survival of the fittest" to describe the effects of the action of natural selection.

Darwin's views were similar to those of an earlier French scientist, Jean-Baptiste de Monet, chavalier de Lamarck (1744-1829), though with an essential difference. Both men claimed that evolution accounted for the differences in the various species, but whereas Darwin held that evolution was the result of the transmission of inborn genetic traits from one generation to another, Lamarck believed that evolution was the result of acquired traits being passed on to progeny. Lamarck's views have been thoroughly discredited. For them to be correct, there would need to be the transmission of acquired capacities in the muscles, tissues, brain cells, and so on, to the actual genes of the individual so that genetic transmission could advance the strengths of the father into the son—something for which no evidence has been forthcoming. It has never been shown that there is a necessary transmission of acquired characteristics from the parents to the offspring. Yet it is important to mention Lamarck, for both the proponents and opponents of the theory of evolution sometimes merge Darwin's and Lamarck's views in the course of arguments for or against evolution. Moreover, even though Darwin's concept of evolution was different from Lamarck's, and though Darwin was not intending to study ultimate origins but merely the differentiation of species, both theories invite a study of ultimate origins and both assume as a given an "other" outside the organism that leads to a change in the organism. Carried back to ultimate origins, both Darwin and Lamarck offer as many questions as they supply answers.

Darwin strongly argued that the evidence of what he called "variation under domestication" was proof of this process of generic change. He argued that if the breeder of a certain species could bring into being changes he preferred (color, size, and so on), then nature could do far better. He wrote an entire chapter on the subject of variation under domestication. He said, for instance, that when we compare the individuals of the same variety or sub-variety of our older cultivated plants and animals, one of the first points which strikes us is that they generally differ more from each other than do the individuals of any one species or variety in a state of nature. And if we reflect on the vast diversity of the plants and animals which have been cultivated and which have varied during all ages under the most different climates and treatment, we are driven to conclude that this great variability is due to our domestic productions having been raised under conditions of life not so uniform as, and somewhat different from, those to which the parent species had been exposed under nature.[8]

Darwin concluded a lengthy discussion of the concept with the interesting observation: "To sum up on the origin of our domestic races of animals and plants, changed conditions of life are of the highest importance in causing variability, both by acting directly on the organization, and indirectly by affecting the reproductive system."[9]

Darwin built many disclaimers and conditions into his argument. He said, for example, that

it is not probable that variability is an inherent and necessary contingent under all circumstances. The greater or less force of inheritance and revision, determine whether variations shall endure. Variability is governed by many unknown laws, of which correlated growth is probably the most important. Something, but how much we do not know, may be attributed to the definite action of the conditions of life. Some, perhaps a great effect, may be attributed to the increased use or disuse of parts. The final result is thus rendered infinitely complex. . . . Over all these causes of Change, the accumulative action of Selection, whether applied methodically and quickly, or unconsciously and slowly but more efficiently, seems to have been the predominant Power.[10]

Darwin was a collector. He collected insects, beetles, flora, and fauna on his trip to the Galapagos on the *Beagle*. He wrote extensively about differences in coloration, shape, size, beak length, and other variations among the birds he observed from one island to another. He used these observations to press the

8. Ibid., p. 31.
9. Ibid., p. 57.
10. Ibid., p. 57.

assumption that the mysterious force called *natural selection* had produced these differences.

In later life, Darwin raised pigeons and observed their development closely. Also, he paid great attention to various flowers in his garden and assembled what he called "data" from those observations. In fact, so numerous were Darwin's observations and so voluminous was his data that the sheer weight of his writings tended to be a part of the proof of his contention for the survival of the fittest.

The world of the natural sciences was impressed. It is almost as if the scientists were waiting for such a view. However, the scientists so impressed with Darwin's theory seemed to forget or ignore the fact that no way presently exists whereby data from the present can prove, of itself, anything about ultimate origins. Proof, to live up to its name, must mean demonstrating that something we do not know conforms exactly to something we do know. Consequently, there is simply nothing we know either by observation or through logical proof concerning the origin of individual species or the origin of life itself. Our observations in the present are exactly that—*present* data. What we think they tell us about the past are subjective considerations. They cannot be held to be science at all.

In considering Darwin's theory, we find ourselves curious about this thing called a *species*.

What really is a species? This question bedeviled Darwin all his life, and it has not, in fact, been answered to this very day. It is a simple fact of science that no two things anywhere are exactly alike. There are no two birds, elephants, eyes, feet, claws, or feathers that can be declared alike by the standards of provable science. Similarities are there, but everyone knows that similarities often prove to be embarrassingly superficial. Mistaken identity due to "similarity" is an experience common to us all.

A *species* in the field of science, therefore, has never been exactly defined. Even the most modern scientific journals discuss this fact only when forced to, and then only under the most general terms. One can therefore easily argue that a *species* exists only by human definition and not in exactly provable objective fact. Darwin himself said, "I was much struck how entirely

vague and arbitrary is the distinction between species and vari-
eties."[11] In fact, Darwin suggested the methodology to decide the
matter of species:

> Hence, in determining whether a form should be ranked as a
> species or a variety, the opinion of naturalists having sound judg-
> ment and wide experience seems *the only guide to follow*. We
> must, however, in many cases, decide by a majority of naturalists,
> for a few well-marked and well-known varieties can be named
> which have not been ranked as species by at least some compe-
> tent judges.[12]

What do we have here? An entire book built around the
word *species*, which word can only be defined by a vote of the
naturalists. Appropriate comment could be made to this methodology, but it at least demonstrates that the idea of species and
their origins is built on troubled logic, inexact science, and the
absence of clear definitions.

Really, then, is "the doctrine of the survival of the fittest"
true? This amounts to what is well called "the law of the
jungle."

But when we think about it, *there is no law of the jungle*.

The rule, it is said, that obtains in the jungle is that the
strong overcome the weak. The strong, therefore, survive, and
the weak become fodder for the strong. With the help of Darwin,
this rule was dignified by being called *natural selection*.

Mind you, Darwin called this a *law*.

Darwin professed to have "seen," indeed discovered, this
"law" when he proceeded to elevate it to an axiom of life. Because biology is destiny for many, this "principle" has become
for them the law of life. Whatever we may say, this is the way it
is in the thinking of most people.

But is this the way it really is? We submit to each thinking
person that this is *not* the way it is. The argument against it is
painfully simple: if the law of the jungle were indeed a law, if
the survival of the fittest were the way it is, there then would be
only one being on earth—the strongest—and that not for long.

11. Ibid., p. 63.
12. Ibid., p. 62.

Let us think about this.

The male of the species is normally stronger than the female, and is therefore more fit. Under the law of the jungle, the male should kill the female, and that would be that. The lion would kill the lioness. Soon there would be no more cubs, and if there were, the lion would kill them too.

"But no!" the Darwinist would say. "The law of natural selection is conditioned by 'filial forbearance.' You just don't eat your relatives."

But still, what about the strong lion killing all the females and the cubs of another lion family? "They are protected by the strong lion of that family." Why, then, does not that strong lion eat the cubs and females of the first family? Here the Darwinist would say that natural selection is conditioned not between individuals but within a species.

Why does not the strong lion eat *all* the jackals, elephants, or zebras? "These are fast runners." But that is not true when they are asleep or when they are drinking at the water hole. The lions *do* eat *some* of those. "Aha!" says the Darwinist. "They do not eat them *all* because they are not always hungry."

So, another condition of the law is "the presence of hunger."

The "variations" to this law, as we see, go on and on.

For instance, we may be sure that some animals have died by desiccation in a drought, by hunger in a famine, or by heat in a fire. Some, even the strong, are still here only because they lived in a different part of the jungle when the flames came, or because they didn't get bitten by a spider when another did.

Yes, so many conditioning factors make for survival that we must see that it is not possible to name a *constant*, a *law* concerning the matter of survival. Accident, sickness, surprise, falling trees, lightning strikes, stray bullets, and a thousand other variables impinge upon the life of any animate thing. In fact, a near infinity of conditioning factors is present. So many are there that the argument dissolves into absurdity.

Therefore, there is no animal or species of which one can say with certainty, "He will survive. He is the strongest." The only way to define a survivor is to point to those individuals and species that have, in fact, survived. Therefore, the argument, being circuitous, is false. The *survival of the fittest* only means the *survival of the survivors.* A survivor can only be defined *ex post facto.* Therefore, to make *natural selection* the determining factor in history is to make a false assumption. And even if the assumption were true, it could not be *proved* to be true.

Circuitous arguments are common fallacies, but initially they are sometimes unrecognized because the circle is too large to be observed by some minds all at one time.

So obvious is this that one wonders why science has become the object of such wide and uncritical respect. It even now sees itself as the custodian of the great truths that matter. The broad, largely unquestioned acceptance of Darwinism by "the world of science" and "the men of science" is a present condition that should not go unchallenged.

The circuitous arguments on which Darwinism and other of the axioms of science are built have become virtually foundational in modern education. In this, there is great peril to the culture of our time. The modern mind must force itself to rethink what it means when it speaks of this great, all-pervading, and sure knowledge that is called *science.*

2
Thinking Further About Science

As we have noticed, Darwin presented the concept of natural selection as the latest discovery, even a *law* of science. The initial impact of Darwin's research was upon the scientific community of his day, but that influence continues to be felt in the reverence the scientific community of our day gives to Darwin's ideas. It is useful, therefore, for us to consider this matter we call *science* and to investigate what we mean by the term. For indeed, science has come to be thought of as a mysterious entity beyond the intellectual capabilities of the average man; it is assumed that only rarely are the mysterious inner chambers of science penetrated by ordinary people.

In the word *scientist* we have one of the most revered titles of our day, because the word denotes one of the most respected professions of modern times. It might even be argued that modern times have themselves been created by the phenomena denoted in the phrase *the advance of science*. Science and the scientist have taken to themselves credentials deemed unassailable in our culture.

So much is this the case that any finding about anything can be rendered instantly déclassé by tagging it with the criti-

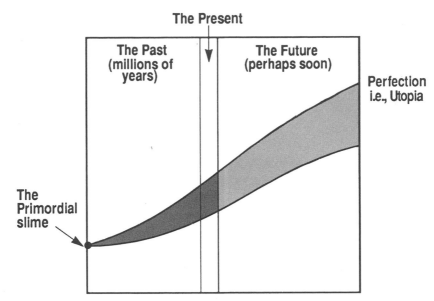

Fig. 1. What the scientist thinks he sees in viewing history

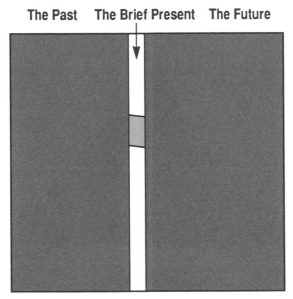

Fig. 2. What the scientist really sees

cism "It's not scientific." On the other hand, the sublime truth of almost anything is established instantly when the expression "Science has taught us" is applied to it. "Being scientific" is to travel the high road of acceptance and status. So pervasive is this assumption that many strange notions have gained credibility when their proponents have applied to them the term *scientific*. The status of being "scientific" is so desired today that the word *science* has been inflated to the point that it is assumed that science knows it all and can tell us anything. Our society has come to assume that the source of all knowledge is science; once a thing is established as being scientific, it moves beyond debate and becomes an article of faith.

But what are we really talking about when we refer to "what science has done" and talk about how science will bring to pass a new and better world? Is it not possible that when we think a little more deeply about science we shall discover that science is valuable only to a certain point, after which it becomes a false legitimizer of a whole set of unwarranted and dangerous conclusions?

What is science? At its core, science is observation. What distinguishes that observation from the normal apprehension of things is that it is a more careful, more codified, more patiently recorded observation than merely the casual observations of life.

What does science observe? First of all, and most basically, science observes *entities*. Science says, "This is a rock." Upon deeper observation, science says, "This is granite," or, "This is sandstone." It moves from superficial to analytical observation. It tells us specifically what kind of a rock this is. In its function as an observer, science has discovered and related information about the elements that constitute the components of the things that·can, in limited fashion, be observed.

Second, science observes *combinations of entities*. Science tells us, "This rock and that moss usually go together," or, "This thunder and this lightning often are present in combination." It tells us that air is composed of oxygen, nitrogen, and trace elements.

Third, science observes *phenomena*. It notices, for example, that when sodium and water come together the result is the springing up of fire. Phenomena, therefore, are normally matter

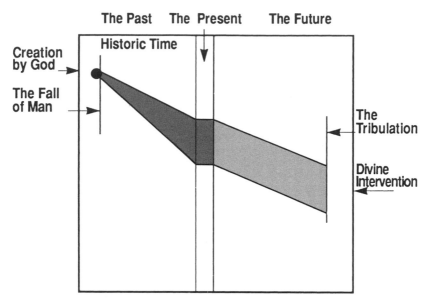

Fig. 3. The actual course of history as it has transpired and will unfold

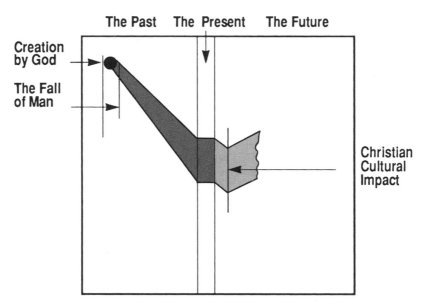

Fig. 4. The exception to cultural deterioration

in motion, matter changing its form, or matter moving from the apparently inert to the dynamic.

Fourth, science *performs experiments.* It sets up laboratories and brings together certain entities that do not combine predictably in nature. By making these combinations predictable, science can observe even more deeply the phenomena that can be produced by artificially bringing together certain combinations of elements. The controlled experiment is science's most dependable device for proper observation.

At its core, then, science is empiricism. It *observes* things and attempts to state the facts about the essence of those things and about the observable activity that those things produce when they are related to other things in certain quantities and environments.

Having observed and analyzed, science moves into the realm of the practical, suggesting valuable new combinations that are of practical use in the world beyond the laboratory. In this commendable function, science has given us the internal combustion engine, the flashlight, the rocket, the space shuttle, the satellite, radio transmission, and a thousand other dependable products that once would have been the astonishment of society. Even now, out of its experiments, science produces products whose unforeseen capabilities are the wonderment of us. The careful observation of things (entities) and phenomena (matter in interaction) has produced a myriad of useful discoveries that have given the illumination, mobility, and efficiency to major sections—specifically to the civilized portion—of the human race. These wonders have produced a predictable, even legitimate, well-earned respect for the observations and applications of those millions of patient workers in our time called *scientists.*

That respect has now, however, led society into a dangerous attitude, an attitude that comes close to making a god out of science. This unwise apotheosis should concern thinking people. A timely warning concerning the limitations of science needs to be raised, for no one is truly wise or scientific unless he knows not only the possibilities but also the impossibilities of science. One would do well, then, to think about the limitations of science.

1. *Science cannot know the ultimate nature of things.* Observation and analysis can take us only so far. After that there stretches out, beyond our ability to observe, the unreachable vistas of a limitless unknown. Despite its accomplishments, science has given us no final answers. No one knows what life is. No one knows what light is. No one knows what the final building blocks of matter are. No one knows how the mind influences the body. Scientists deal with electricity, but no one knows what electricity is. We know something about phenomena, but we do not know anything about the ontology of things. We know what things *do,* but we do not know what things *are.*

2. *Science cannot know the origin of things.* We know of the present existence of certain entities and phenomena, but the *provenance* of these things escapes us. The assertion that something was created or brought to pass *ex nihilo* (out of nothing) is an assertion about which science is unable to comment. No observer of anything can tell us the origin of that thing solely on the basis of observation. Whether or not the universe was created out of nothing is a question that the scientist, as a scientist, has no more competence to answer than an ordinary man. When Charles Darwin wrote *Origin of the Species* he told us nothing about origins. Rather he spoke only of processes through which he believed biological life replicated itself upward, successive generations reproducing from the simple to the complex. But this theory was arbitrarily distilled from his observation of present life forms and residues. It was not based on empirical observation, for no observer but God was present to observe the beginning of things. The scientist who says, "This is the way it all began," is not speaking as a scientist, but rather as a speculator on a par with all others who speculate about beginnings.

3. *Science cannot fathom past processes.* The function of science is observation of the *present.* One who observes and then thinks that he properly interprets the processes of the present has not thereby taken to himself the credentials of a geological historian, making sure pronouncements about the past. Indeed, the reality we see today may have been brought to pass by a process entirely different from what we think ("what we think" being the results of empirical observation) to be the pres-

ent processes. It is also true that the time element we assume from present processes may not, in fact, have obtained with reference to the past. No one, therefore, can know the age of anything if he was not present to observe that object's beginning or does not have access to someone who was. No one can know with certainty the process from point A to point B unless he has had the opportunity to constantly observe that process or has access to someone who did. Remember, even observation is superficial. Processes, even in the present, vary greatly under the influence of many known and possibly many more unknown conditioning factors.

To say, therefore, that the theory of evolution is scientific is to deprive the word *scientific* of any meaning, for scientific knowledge has to do with observation and experiment. So-called knowledge of a thing like evolution comes neither by observation or experiment and therefore cannot be called scientific. Anyone who is not a fool (a fool being one who willy-nilly changes the meaning of words) should know this.

"But," says the scientist, "evolution is the most *probable* account of the past." But, alas, here the logic breaks down again. Nothing can be called probable unless it is tested against that which is provable. Without provabilities there are no probabilities. Hence, when he insists that evolution is true, the scientist loses his credentials as a scientist and as a logician.

4. *Science cannot predict the future with certainty.* Being limited to observation and analysis of the present, the true scientist learns to deal very carefully and, we trust, humbly, with the future. After he has made all of the calculations and has constructed all of the models of probability with reference to the future, the scientist dares not truly trust his conclusions apart from experiments. The new plane must be flown by a test pilot— or, better still, a robot—before it carries passengers. The nuclear bomb must be tested at Los Alamos before it is carried on an aircraft to a distant Hiroshima.

No developmental scientist has ever had anything work ex-*actly* as he predicted. Most devices, however careful may have been the process of their development, are failures initially because of some unforeseen element. So the trustworthy scientist will only tentatively suggest the near-term results of a given action, while all of the time keeping his fingers crossed that it will indeed come to pass. Because it so often does not, the scientist learns to leave room in his plans for new and previously unforeseen numbers. The wise scientist asserts little about the future and even less about the past. The future will confirm or deny his experiments; the past retains its stony, stoical silence.

5. *Science cannot control all possible forces.* The wise scientist admits that he must deal with "the powers that be." He is not the Creator but, rather, is a myopic, observing creature. He did not create gravity and does not really know what it is. In his experiments he merely creates minuscule, controlled situations and hopes for the best. Even these situations tend to teach him that he is not an originator or an actuator but is instead a cooperator with vast realities that are beyond his comprehension.

No mind in all the earth can prove that it *knows* what are *all* the forces that work upon us at any given moment. Because we know the ultimate nature of nothing, we must therefore content ourselves with a few feeble measurements of our present condition and use those measurements in our crude experiments. Even while doing the measuring, we must, if we are properly humble, admit to the possible existence of a hundred other forces that are beyond our ability to measure. When speaking about anything—about space, for example—the competent scientist can be heard to say, "There may be a thousand other things out there about which we know nothing, and we are curious to examine them." Curiosity rather than foolish over-confidence is the proper attitude of the scientist.

So it is that the casualties of the space shuttle or the victims of the San Francisco earthquake should produce within all of us the proper degree of humility. The presence of casualty in the universe is irrefutable, settle-it-forever evidence that man is not the master, but only the observer. The idea that the individual man is the true master of anything is finally unforgivable self-idolatry.

6. *Science cannot know the reason "Why?"* When the child asks, "Why does the sun come up in the morning?" we think we have the answer, indeed have said something profound, by talking about the rotation of the earth. In the same fashion, science pretends to have the answer by saying that the warming winds

in the south come from the *el niño* factor. The scientist explains summer, winter, spring, and fall by speaking of the orbit of the earth around the sun and the degree of tilt in the earth's axis that makes it appear that the sun moves north and south of the equator. With quickly spoken words like these, the scientist thinks that he has explained the seasons. But the questions remain: "*Why* does the earth tilt?" "*Why* does the sun shine at that exact intensity?"

The scientist can be expected to be impatient with, even embarrassed by, these questions. That is because he knows that they point to a process called "infinite regression." Behind all questions are deeper questions, and behind those are deeper ones yet. Therefore, the question, "Why?" can only be answered superficially in a way that we hope will satisfy the curiosity of the moment.

But ultimate answers escape us. Any person who hopes to retain his sanity must never forget that basic fact: ultimate answers escape us. This is true about every person, however brilliant and insightful he may be, from Albert Einstein (who never found the unified field theory, the quest of his lifetime) to the most immature school child. The simple fact is that ultimate answers have not been and cannot be discovered by scientific research. The things that can be seen by the eye only reveal, and that fractionally, something of their nature and their activities. The rationale behind that nature and the true engine behind that observable activity cannot be divined by any mere observation.

7. *Science cannot say what ought to be.* In all of its observations, science is really discovering what *is*, or what *happens*. Science as such has nothing to say about "oughtness," the idea that one thing is right and another thing wrong. It simply observes and makes humble suggestions as to probabilities that may or may not be confirmed about the activity of physical entities in the near future. That's it.

Moreover, whereas ultimate things are not made of atoms and molecules, it is precisely and only with physical entities that science concerns itself. Thus, for answers to questions of ultimate meaning one has to go beyond science.

So, again, science as such cannot tell us what to do. It is unable to suggest the key to happiness, purpose, or fulfillment.

It knows nothing of intangibles such as love, hate, honor, duty, or even valid ambitions. Being unable to discuss what most people understand to be spiritual things, science bows out.

It follows, therefore, that we ought not to make a god out of science. It is far more limited, inarticulate, and mute as to the realities of life than most people realize. Science is, in its real sense, a mechanical, undramatic thing. Yes, it occasionally ignites a fire, but men must not mistake that fire for the true and worthy object of their worship. Science is basically "nuts and bolts" (or the modern counterpart) and should be respected for what it is, but it should not be revered.

How, then, shall we discover the realities of the distant past, the infinite future, the remoteness of space, or the inner reaches of the soul? How shall we know who to love, who to hate, what to live for, what to die for? Why should a man be true to his wife or do the honest thing rather than the convenient thing? Why are some things worth dying for and others of little or no value? Yes, where do values come from, and how do they apply to life?

Science is unable to provide an answer to these and other important questions of life. As far as science is concerned, a hatchet is a hatchet, whether it is used to carve a statue or to kill a friend.

But, alas, we learn from departments other than science that a hatchet is not just a hatchet. It is an instrument capable of being used for moral or immoral purposes. We instantly see, therefore (if we are not blinded), that important things are not atoms, molecules, hatchets, or rockets. No, indeed, important things are moral values. Life and existence in this world cannot be explained or appreciated apart from them.

Where do moral values come from? They come from the eternal and everlasting God who made the universe. This is the God whose existence some scientists deny—not because they are scientists but because they lack humility, never having taken the time to properly consider the limitations of science. How supremely ridiculous it is for a person to hold a bubbling test tube up against the sun and say, "There is no God!" Yes, the scientist may have "made" the test tube (he didn't really), but who made the sun? The beginning of wisdom is recognizing that there is a God who stands behind it all. This God created the universe; it is "the work of His hands."

But if science is no help, how can we know this God?

Here science shows its limitations. It can only suggest the first step, the beginning of that quest. It helps us to observe nature, and helps mostly when it states that "this is the creation of God."

The beautiful and complete answer to the question, "How can we know God?" is given to us by God Himself. It is that God made the universe and has revealed Himself in time and space in the Person of Jesus Christ, His only begotten Son. Wisdom begins when we come to know Christ, in whom are hidden all of the treasures of wisdom and knowledge. The created universe, with all of its wonders, is but the backdrop to the real story of eternity, the story of redemption in Christ. Let no one become so preoccupied with so-called science that he neglects to move beyond science with its limitations to a knowledge of the invisible God. Science is neither ultimately nor dependably accurate. It gives us but a superficial analysis of the work of God in creation. The work of God in redemption is the great work of the Lord. He invites every person who lives to believe the gospel, to come to know Christ, and to have the gift of God, which is life eternal.

As we have seen, science cannot explain the moral nature of man, and therefore refuses to recognize the depths of sin into which man has fallen. It sees no need for redemption but only calls for education. Being so disposed, it cannot offer true hope to a lost humanity. It has been very good, however, at producing the instruments by which a lost humanity progressively attempts to destroy itself.

Science attempts to analyze the created universe behind which is God. It is that God who invites us to step up from empiricism to faith. Faith in Christ and the work on the cross is the door to eternal life and ultimate knowledge.

3

Social Darwinism

How, then, does Darwin rule from his grave?

The answer has to do with the questions everyone at some time or another asks: *What makes the world continue? Where did I come from? Why are things as they are?* These are important, perennial questions. Not to ask them is to give evidence of having a mind narrower than the one needed to survive in the world of men and nations. But what is particularly significant in our day is the way these questions have been answered by the intellectually elite.

As is so often the case with an intellectual construct, Darwinism has moved out from its original platform to operate in a wider world. The ideas of evolution have left the confines of biology, botany, and paleontology and are now thought to apply to the social structure at large. This application of Darwinism to social structures is called Social Darwinism and is foundational for our culture. It represents the way Darwin rules our society from the grave.

What are the assumptions that make up this Social Darwinism? The first assumption is the idea that the social structure is engineered and controlled by impersonal forces rather than by

God. Until the emergence of Social Darwinism, it was generally held in the West that the process of history constantly revealed that the Judeo-Christian God was behind it. The founders of America rested in the confidence that "there is a just God who presides above the destinies of nations." That statement revealed the mind-set of Western culture present at the time. It was a largely undisputed first principle in the light of which other realities were examined.

Darwin changed all of this. His idea of natural selection is meaningless gibberish unless he is in fact referring to an impersonal force, a power that propels history and establishes its direction. Although Darwin had Christian associations as a young man, as his life progressed he became less and less willing to ascribe the control and direction of history to God. Rather, he came to think of the progress of history as being determined by the impersonal engine of natural selection. God was exchanged for a force, and history dropped into a depersonalized mode.

The Social Darwinists of our time have continued along this line. Our society, once rightly called a Christian civilization, has become secular to a greater degree than the solons of Western civilization would have thought possible. Education, government, business, the media, and, in many cases, religion, have moved through progressive stages of secularization from Christianity to atheism. As a result, God is not merely ignored but rather is resented, opposed, and vilified at every opportunity. With unimaginable arrogance, our society has declared Jesus Christ to be *persona non grata* in the culture. Concomitantly, the Bible has lost its final authority, the Christian religion has been pluralized, the family is fast disappearing, and morals are at a low ebb. Those who insist that the force that moves history is not God are now on the speaker's platform and before the television cameras. What will they do when the platform collapses and the lights go out?

The second assumption of Social Darwinism is that society is moving upward from a mean past to an improving future. The evolutionist insists that life began in the primordial slime as its lowly provenance. The engine of culture worked from there, producing in our time the best world that has ever been. This "improvement" will continue until perfect culture comes into being.

Social Darwinism is utopian. It looks at what it thinks is a straight upward line of progress from the past until this moment. It then extends that dotted line into the future, implying and directly asserting that that utopia will be produced by the maturing evolutionary process. Although the promise of a perfect tomorrow is a perennial theme of politics, education, commerce, and religion, because of Social Darwinism, our present society has heard more promises along this line than most.

The assertion is even made that evolution has given us the intelligence and technical skill to control our own evolution. So man now becomes some kind of a god. But those who promise inevitable improvement in the social structure are hard put to produce any evidence of that improvement. In fact, by every relevant standard of measurement, we are living not in an improving society but, rather, are living in a deteriorating one.

That is particularly evident when we consider the ultimate standard by which improvement or degeneration of a culture is to be measured, the moral standard. Whatever may be the degree of technical progress or military prowess, those advances are meaningless apart from moral improvement. Technical improvement apart from moral improvement is thus a sure harbinger of fatal consequences. When advancing technology and declining morality occur concurrently, as they do in our time, they become a time bomb capable of blowing history into a thousand pieces. Yet the utopians of our society are so committed to Social Darwinism that they refuse to consider any evidence but the superficial tokens of improvement. This attitude, if continued, will be fatal.

The third assumption of Social Darwinism is that man, a human, is nothing more than a higher sort of animal. This claim is set forth succinctly in the title of a book that popularized the concept, Desmond Morris's *The Naked Ape* (1980). Man is seen as little more than an intelligent orangutan. Those who protest the classification are chided by the social elite for being inconsiderate to their hairy cousins.

Yet it strikes us that the one who holds that the human and the orangutan are related has not spent much time in a zoo. In purely biological terms, the evolutionary connection between man and the animals is unproved by any evidence, although it is continually proclaimed by the social scientists who have become the gurus of our culture. Moreover, Social Darwinism is not able to explain the moral structure of the human being, specifically the fact that man has an acute sense of the difference between *is* and *ought*, a difference that cannot possibly come from chemistry. Science can tell us what has happened, but it is unable to tell us what should have happened or what should not have happened.

The fourth assumption of Social Darwinism is the idea that soul, spirit, and eternal life are but chemical actions of the brain. This kind of chemical determinism refuses to admit the existence of "mind" but holds that all things, even those things considered "thoughts," come from brain matter. Here the evolutionist reveals that he must also be a behaviorist. He must hold that the difference between Shakespeare and some village pornographer is created by accidental connections of cells within the human cortex.

At this point the evolutionary concept breaks down completely. If all things, including human thought and spirituality, are determined by electrochemistry in the human cranium, we have a mechanistic universe. In such a universe, existence is the same as nonexistence, up is not different from down, logic is nonsense, and rationality evaporates before our eyes. Nothing remains but nihilism, where all things never were, never are, nor ever will be. If the mind is not an entity separate and distinct from the physical body, the light of understanding goes out and all becomes incomprehensible.

And who can doubt that incomprehensibility has become the condition of our present age? This world, professing itself to be wise, has become foolish, as the apostle Paul puts it in the book of Romans. It has "changed the glory of the incorruptible God into an image like corruptible man, and birds and four-footed beasts, and creeping things" (1:23). God gives up such to "uncleanness," "vile affections," and a "reprobate mind" (Romans 1:24-28). A world that drops into reprobation has moved beyond hope and beyond life.

As we look about us at the deterioration of our culture, we cannot help but wonder why that deterioration has occurred. A significant part of the answer is that our present age has willingly succumbed to the anti-intellectualism of Social Darwinism. The world that Darwin rules from his grave is not a world of ivory palaces and mounting perfection. No, indeed, it is a world that sees the lowering sun of the afternoon of life without ever remembering that afternoon is succeeded by evening, and evening by night.

Darwin's son described early memories he had of his father: "I remember him many years ago at a christening, a memory which has remained with me, because to us children it seemed an extraordinary and abnormal occurrence. I remember his look most distinctly at his brother Erasmus' funeral, as he stood in the scattering of snow, wrapped in a long black funeral coat, with a grave look of sad revery."[1]

---

1. Charles Darwin, *Charles Darwin's Autobiography* (New York: Henry Schuman, 1950), p. 90.

4

The Ruling Principle for All Humanity: Karl Marx

Beneath the leaden skies north of London met that day a small and sober group of mourners. It was Saturday, March 17, 1883, and the faithful had gathered for the funeral service of the man who was to be called by some the greatest thinker in all of history. The accolades concerning his life and thought border on idolatry, and the promises believed by many as to the future he had created amount to little short of heaven on earth.

The body in the casket was that of Karl Marx.

Who was this man? One of the most expressive answers to that question was contained in the funeral oration made on that occasion by his friend Friedrich Engels. Engels spoke in English to those assembled, and his words are considered one of the best short presentations of the life and work of the man whose body was being placed in the ground.

> On the 14th of March, at a quarter to three in the afternoon, the greatest living thinker ceased to think. He had been left alone for scarcely two minutes, and when we came back, we found him in an armchair, peacefully gone to sleep—but forever.

An immeasurable loss has been sustained, both by the militant *proletariat* of Europe and America, and by historical science, in the death of this man. The gap that has been left by the death of this mighty spirit will soon enough make itself felt.

Just as Darwin discovered the law of evolution in organic nature, so Marx discovered the law of evolution in human history; he discovered the simple fact, hitherto concealed by an overgrowth of ideology, that mankind must first of all eat and drink, have shelter and clothing, before it can pursue politics, science, religion, art, etc.; and that therefore the production of the immediate material means of life and consequently the degree of economic development attained by a given people or during a given epoch, form the foundation upon which the forms of government, the legal conceptions, the art, and even the religious ideas of the people concerned have been evolved, and in the light of which these things must therefore be explained, instead of vice versa as had hitherto been the case.

Engels continued that graveside speech:

But that is not all. Marx also discovered the special law of motion governing the present-day capitalist method of production and the *bourgeois* society that this method of production has created. The discovery of surplus value suddenly threw light on the problem in trying to solve which all previous investigators, both *bourgeois* economists and socialist critics, had been groping in the dark.

Two such discoveries would be enough for one life-time. Happy the man to whom it is granted to make even one such discovery. But in every single field which Marx investigated—and he investigated very many fields, none of them superficially—in every field, even in that of mathematics, he made independent discoveries.

This was the man of science. But this was not even half the man. Science was for Marx a historical, dynamic, revolutionary force. However great the joy with which he welcomed a new discovery in some theoretical science whose practical application perhaps it was as yet quite impossible to envisage, he experienced a quite other kind of joy when the discovery involved immediate revolutionary changes in industry and in the general course of history. For example, he followed closely the discoveries made in the field of electricity and recently those of Marcel Deprez.

Here Engels reveals the real Marx:

> For Marx was before all else a revolutionary. His real mission in life was to contribute in one way or another to the overthrow of capitalist society and of the forms of government which it had brought into being, to contribute to the liberation of the present-day proletariat, which he was the first to make conscious of its own position and its needs, of the conditions under which it could win its freedom. Fighting was his element. He fought with a passion, a tenacity, and a success such as few could rival. His work on the first *Rheinische Zeitung* (1842), the *Paris Vorwarts* (1844), the *Brussels Deutsche Zeitung* (1847), the *Neue Rheinische Zeitung* (1848-9), the *New York Tribune* (1852-61), and in addition to these, a host of militant pamphlets, work in revolutionary clubs in Paris, Brussels, and London, and finally, crowning all, the formation of the International Working Men's Association—this was indeed an achievement of which Marx might well have been proud, even if he had done nothing else.
>
> And consequently, Marx was the best-hated and most-calumniated man of his time. Governments, both absolutist and republican, deported him from their territories. The *bourgeoisie*, whether conservative or extreme Democrat, vied with one another in heaping slanders upon him. All this he brushed aside as if it were cobweb, ignoring them, answering only when necessity compelled him. And now he has died—beloved, revered, and mourned by millions of revolutionary fellow-workers—from the mines of Siberia to California, in all parts of Europe and America—and I make bold to say though he may have opponents he has hardly one personal enemy.
>
> His name and his work will endure through the ages![1]

This eulogy came from the pen of the man who was the closest associate of Karl Marx through the course of his adult life. We can therefore conclude that this speech represents the way Marx and his work was understood by his followers and the degree of influence he and they hoped would result in the world outside of their immediate circle.

The same sentiment as Engels's is expressed by Philip Foner in the preface to an elaborate collection of responses to the death of Karl Marx called *Karl Marx Remembered:*

---

1. Philip Foner, *Karl Marx Remembered* (San Francisco: Synthesis, 1983), p. 38.

Marxism is today the most influential body of thought in the world. Hundreds of millions live in societies whose fundamental principles—socialism—were laid down over a century ago by Karl Marx and his collaborator and friend, Friedrich Engels. Both were Germans, but they propounded principles that were and remain universal and international. The universality and internationalism of Marxism have been demonstrated again and again from the moment it came into existence, and one of the manifestations of its international character was evident in the mourning which followed the news that on March 14, 1883, Karl Marx, the father of socialism, had died. Coupled with the grief was the universal respect for the enormous contributions this man made to mankind.[2]

Foner also asserts: "I am confident that when the two hundredth anniversary of the death of Karl Marx will be observed, the entire world will be socialist."[3]

More than a few books could be filled with the eulogistic quotations of the followers—indeed the worshipers—of Karl Marx, using the most complimentary language imaginable to refer to him and the contribution he made to society.

Yes, it could be argued that the world-changing effect of the life and philosophy of Karl Marx is a measurable thing, and by that measure he has been one of the greatest influences in history.

That simple measure testifies that the philosophy of Karl Marx and the political structure that grew from his work has conquered and presently controls one-third of the population of the world. For most of the era following World War II, Communism has been the form of political ideology and consequent government in iron control over the lives and fortunes of one-and-a-half billion people. From 1918 onward, no major international political decision has been made by any power in the world apart from the question, What will Russia and the Communists think of this?

A second form of influence beside political control has been exercised by the ghost of Karl Marx. That is the control that comes about when ideas are extended into a belief structure that

2. Ibid., p. 10.
3. Ibid., p. 18.

dominates the minds of men. The belief structure of Marxism can surely be said to be a dominant feature over another third of the world. The portion of earth we call the Third World is highly Marxist in nature. Western societies have not been exempt, either, for particularly on the academic level, multitudes have been in thrall to Marxism.

Who was this man whose ideas made such an impact in the past and who continues to a high degree to rule the world from his grave?

A minimum definition would call Karl Marx a social philosopher from Germany, born of Jewish parents, and highly influenced by the radical ideas that made an impact upon him in his youth. Marx was born on May 5, 1818, to what would be called a generally upper-class German family. His father was a lawyer of Jewish background who converted from Judaism to Lutheranism in 1817. Some of Marx's biographers suggest that this conversion stemmed more from practicality than from conviction, thereby leading to the suggestion that religion was at the background of the Marx family rather than at its core.

Still, in his early life Marx considered the possibility of entering the Lutheran ministry, and he attended a religious preparatory school for a time. Some of the writings of this aspiring young man remain in which he discussed Christ, Christianity, and the gospel. One gets the impression, however, that he was writing as a young academic observer rather than as a participant in the Christian religion. He studied law at both Bonn and Berlin, but in the process of his education became more interested in abstract philosophy than in the practice of law. He took a Ph.D. degree in 1842 at Jena, where the requirements expected of doctoral candidates were less stringent than they were in Berlin.

In those days, Europe was a place of animated intellectual interaction, with various schools of thought developing around many points of view having to do with the purpose of life, the nature of government, and the engines of history. The ideas of Hegel were much in discussion across Europe. In noting these discussions, we can observe an early exhibition of Marx's reactionary tendencies, for though Marx retained some of the dialectic concepts of Hegel, he rebelled against Hegel's idealistic emphasis and instead embraced the materialism of Ludwig Feuerbach as a philosophy by which life should be lived.

In 1842, Marx began to express not only his growing literary abilities but also his radicalism by becoming the editor of *Rheinische Zeitung.* From that point throughout the rest of his life, Marx was not content simply to give pallid interpretations of the news and the ideas of his time. Rather, he used his verbal abilities to shock and unsettle his readers, calling for radical reforms in the government, reforms the government thought too bizarre to allow Marx to continue advocating. Consequently, the newspaper was suppressed after but a year of publication.

Indignant over this rejection, Marx migrated to Paris, which he considered to be more hospitable to revolutionary ideas and more willing to shelter the malcontents of the world. After all, Paris in the 1840s was still recovering from the seismic shock of the French Revolution. Those drastic days of revolution, in which the social structure of Paris, France, and Europe was torn to shreds, could not avoid becoming the continuing subject of discussion by intellectuals in France and throughout Europe. To this day the French Revolution is viewed by the nations of the West with a kind of strange fascination coupled with horror. At the same time this bloody event is incorporated into Communist thought as a proud part of the heritage of Communist movements throughout the world.

Starting with an inchoate set of political ideas, the French Revolution thrashed its way into revolutionary political activity and then massive military campaigns that were to consume the lives of perhaps 4 million of the sons of Europe. The most notable aspect of the French Revolution is that it created the kind of man who had not seriously existed on earth before.

This new kind of man was the professional revolutionary.

The professional revolutionary is the radical individual who, while disbelieving in God, soul, and eternal destiny, is still willing to hazard his life to produce revolutionary change. The professional revolutionary is possibly the world's most dangerous man.

Marx knew, and the thinkers of that time knew, that behind the terrors of the French Revolution was the philosophy articulated by Jean Jacques Rousseau (1712-78). Rousseau contended that the progress of the sciences and the arts had actually contributed to the corruption of humanity rather than to its improvement. Put another way, Rousseau rejected the doctrine of original sin and held instead that it was the advance of civilization that had corrupted society. Therefore, civilization, as represented by capitalism, royal government, and a long-established church, needed to be rejected. Man must immerse himself in a back-to-nature movement.

The mature Rousseau then took to analyzing government and concluded that the lone acceptable form of government was the one that would come to pass on the basis of a "social contract" between the citizens and the government. Reasonable men were entirely able to form a compact with one another that would do away with the forms of corruption other analysts of history have called *sin*. Righteous men were the answer, Rousseau asserted, defining righteous people as those who lived as he did and embraced his points of view. The trouble is that Rousseau was a perfectly despicable character. He fathered five illegitimate children by his semiliterate mistress, Thérèse le Vasseur, which children he then sent off to die in the local children's "hospital."

The ideas of Rousseau quickly matured into the grievous scenes of the French Revolution. Those fearful days demonstrated for all to see that man was not essentially righteous, good, and charitable. Rather, they gave evidence that man has a lower nature, which, if given free reign, could turn him into a monster. Indeed, in the revolutionary days of 1789, human monsters owned the streets of Paris. They used the pike and the guillotine to speak to their enemies—and to many of their friends.

Those fearful, revolutionary days, succeeded by the reign of Napoleon Bonaparte, went a long way in producing the France, the Paris, of the nineteenth century. And that is where Marx now chose to live.

It is interesting to note that President Gorbachev of the Soviet Union, while speaking in the United States in 1989, referred to the great heritage of Communism. He announced that the glorious accomplishments of the socialist world revolution were based on two great events in history. Those he identified as the French Revolution of 1789 and the Russian Revolution of 1917.

We hardly need to remind ourselves that these were two of the cruelest political earthquakes in the history of the world. We ought not, therefore, to take lightly a person or nation that still holds those revolutions as a sacred part of their heritage.

It was in Paris in the 1840s that Marx began his lifelong friendship with Friedrich Engels. At the same time, Marx became a socialist and began to pay careful attention to the socialist writers of that day. We do well to wonder what took place in the mind of Karl Marx during those years as he formed his doctrines of "scientific socialism." In some coffee shop, some beer parlor, some darkened library, Marx conceived the notion that has since become fatal to millions. He fancied himself as discovering certain "laws" within the social structure that produce the inevitable advance of socialism. He called this set of laws the "socialist world revolution" and developed the idea that the destiny of the world was at stake in the implementation of those laws for all men and for all nations. The "discovery" of the laws of history, which he saw as working inevitably in the advancement of culture, became a flame within the soul of self-absorbed and impressionable Karl Marx.

So it was that in 1847 he joined the Communist League where, not surprisingly to us, he soon became its leader. Commissioned by the League to bring to the world an expression of its ideas, Marx, along with his friend Engels, penned and published the now famous *Communist Manifesto*. A look at the Manifesto is instructive for the person who would attempt to fathom the reason for the influence of Communism.

Marx opened this fiery piece by saying:

> A specter is haunting Europe—the specter of Communism. All the powers of old Europe have entered into a holy alliance to exorcise this specter; Pope and Czar, *Metternich* and *Guizot*, French Radicals and German police-spies.
>
> It is high time that Communists should openly, in the face of the whole world, publish their views, their aims, their tendencies, and meet this nursery tale of this Specter of Communism with a Manifesto of the party itself.
>
> To this end, Communists of various nationalities have assembled in London, and sketched the following Manifesto, to be

published in the English, French, German, Italian, Flemish, and Danish languages.[4]

Then follows seventy-five pages of invective against the establishment and the announcement that revolutionary socialism would come inexorably, inevitably upon the world.

In the *Manifesto* Marx ascribes all of the cruelties and grievances of history to an entity he calls the *bourgeoisie*. By *bourgeoisie*, Marx means capitalists, the owners of the means of social production and employers of wage-labor. By *proletariat*, he means the class of modern wage-laborers who, having no means of production of their own, are reduced to selling their labor-power in order to live.

Marx inveighs against those who own the means of production, saying, "The *bourgeoisie* has stripped of its halo every occupation hitherto honored and looked upon with reverent awe. It has converted the physician, the lawyer, the priest, the poet, the man of science, into its paid wage-laborers.

"The *bourgeoisie* has torn away from the family its sentimental veil, and has reduced the family relation to a mere money relation."[5]

In the *Manifesto* Marx speaks of the steps by which the Communists intend to bring to pass their goal of "revolutionizing the mode of production":

1) Abolition of property and land and application of all rents of land to public purposes.

2) A heavy progressive or graduated income tax.

3) Abolition of all right of inheritance.

4) Confiscation of the property of all emigrants and rebels.

5) Centralization of credit in the hands of the state by means of a national bank with state capital and an exclusive monopoly.

6) Centralization of the means of communication and the means of transport in the hands of the state.

7) Extension of factories and instruments of production owned by the state; the bringing into cultivation of waste lands,

4. Karl Marx, *The Communist Manifesto*, Gateway Edition (Chicago: Henry Regnery, 1954), pp. 11-12.
5. Ibid., p. 19.

and the improvement of the soil generally in accordance with a common plan.

8)   Equal liability of all to labor. Establishment of industrial armies, especially for agriculture.

9)   Combination of agriculture with manufacturing industries; gradual abolition of the distinction between town and country, by a more equitable distribution of population over the country.

10)   Free education for all children in public schools. Abolition of children's factory labor in its present form. Combination of education with industrial production, etc.[6]

He then promises: "When, in the course of development, class distinctions have disappeared, and all production has been concentrated in the hands of a vast association of the whole nation, the public power will lose its political character."[7]

Marx then makes a utopian promise:

If the *proletariat* during its contest with the *bourgeoisie* is compelled, by the force of circumstances, to organize itself as a class; if, by means of revolution, it makes itself the ruling class, and, as such sweeps away by force the old conditions of production, then it will, along with these conditions, have swept away the conditions for the existence of class antagonisms, and of classes generally, and will thereby have established its own supremacy as a class.

In place of the old *bourgeois* society, with its classes and class antagonisms, we shall have an association, in which the free development of each is the condition for the free development of all.[8]

Time and space would fail to repeat all the demands and promises made by Marx in the *Manifesto*. But it is useful to observe the famous conclusion to the *Manifesto:*

The Communists disdain to conceal their views and aims. They openly declare that their ends can be attained only by the forcible overthrow of all existing social conditions. Let the ruling

6. Ibid., p. 55.
7. Ibid., p. 56.
8. Ibid., pp. 56-57.

classes tremble at a Communist revolution. The *proletarians* have nothing to lose but their chains. They have a world to win!
Working men of all countries, unite![9]

We would do well to remember that Europe in 1848 was in a revolutionary mood. A number of the nations of Europe were in the process of destabilizing themselves. Therefore, the suggestion made by Marx that the true division of society was between the *bourgeoisie* and the *proletariat*—the ruling class and the working class—fell on responsive ears. There can be no doubt that a pro-socialist percolation took place across Europe—in France, Germany, Russia, England, and Italy. Communist parties, by one name or another, began to develop in these lands of Europe and did not neglect to plant the seeds of revolution in the United States. Marx saw himself as the instigator of these changes. So, finally, did the world.

Ideological success is a heady wine indeed.

When one sees his ideas begin to take root in the lives of a few others, he finds it difficult to resist the aspiration to do and say more. Marx was no exception.

Over the next fifteen years he and his friend Engels expended themselves in speech-making, publishing, organizing, and especially in writing on behalf of the coming socialist world revolution. Encouraged by the response to the *Manifesto*, they buried themselves in the cause of establishing Marx's theory of economics and in producing page after page of authoritative-sounding pronouncements as to how that theory would work out in practice.

The result of their efforts was a major work on economics, *Das Kapital*, which appeared in 1867. This book was the first part of a three-volume work edited by Engels. Thus it was that from 1867 forward the world was given massive doses of economic theory far more extensive in sheer volume than anything that had come before. *Das Kapital* was in a quantitative sense so far ahead of any other book of its time that it simply blanked out the competition. The economically minded of the populace reeled under the wagonload of Marx's economic thought. So

9. Ibid., pp. 81-82.

great was the effort of assimilating the massive volume of impassioned ideas that the economic community hardly had time to recover from its effects when along came volumes 2 and 3 of *Das Kapital*, and the smothering effect began again.

No one can deny that the publication of *Das Kapital* had a stunning effect on social and economic thought. Some even called the book "the greatest ever written," and Marx was idolized as an economic thinker who stood on a mountaintop of intellectual insight far above the *petit bourgeoisie* intellectuals of his time—the same view, incidentally, Marx had of himself.

In the sixteen years between the publication of *Das Kapital* and the end of his life, Marx continued to live the life of a near-recluse, his hermitage being the royal library of England. At the same time, his theories of scientific socialism made their way across the world. One can appreciate the impact he made on many individuals by noting some of the remarks published on the occasion of his death in 1883. The *New York Sun* said:

> Karl Marx was by far the best-known, most influential, and intellectually the ablest of those *katheder sozialisten*, or highly educated reformers who in Germany have scrutinized the assumptions and deductions of the orthodox political economists from a new point of view.
>
> If the title of prophet and protagonist belongs to any of the promoters of the world socialist movement, it would by the consent of all intelligent observers be awarded to Karl Marx.

Freiheit said: "On 14 March in London at the age of 65, the greatest thinker of his century, the father of modern socialism, the trailblazer of a new science, the founder of the international working men's association, a hero of the socialist revolution, died—Karl Marx.

"From his grave comes the call which for 40 years he constantly hurled to the world: '*Proletarians* of all countries, unite!'"

The *Boston Daily Advertiser* said: "Karl Marx was one of the most remarkable men of our time, although he lived in comparative obscurity, and his principal work, on Capital, is a special plea rather than an inductive or philosophic treatise."

The *Chicago Tribune* called him "a man of high intelligence, a scholar, and a thinker."

It is obvious, therefore, that the influence of Karl Marx extended into the years following his life. And as we have seen, he continues to hold a major influence in our time, ruling from his grave. Why is this the case?

Why indeed? How is one to explain the fact that nations have been captured by his philosophy and that millions of people, many of them willingly, have marched to their deaths on many battlefields in order to be true to his cause?

We may be helped in answering that question by first asking the basic question, What is Communism? That is because it is Communism that gave us the socialist world revolution and that continues to press upon the intellectual elements of our society its continued call to change the world.

Communism is first of all *atheism*. At the core of its philosophy and conduct is the conviction and the oft-repeated announcement "There is no God."

We must therefore remind ourselves that the declaration of the absence of God is not simply another acceptable philosophic point of view among many others. Rather, it is the denial of the Christian claim—yes, the teaching of the Bible—that there is a just, holy, loving, and personal God who has created the universe and who presides over its continuance. Obviously, there are many implications of such a view, and the Bible is not silent concerning these implications, these dreadful consequences. The Psalmist has told us:

> The fool hath said in his heart, "There is no God." They are corrupt, they have done abominable works, there is none that doeth good. The Lord looked down from heaven upon the children of men, to see if there were any that did understand, and seek God. They are all gone aside, they are all together become filthy; there is none that doeth good, no not one. (Psalm 14:1-3)

This penetrating discourse on the implications of atheism continues by saying, "Have all the workers of iniquity no knowledge, who eat up my people as they eat bread, and call not upon the Lord? There were they in great fear; for God is in the generation of the righteous" (Psalm 14:4-5).

We learn from the Bible, then, that atheism is the philosophy of a fool. It is the emanation of an unsound mind. It is not a philosophy; rather, it is one of the forms of insanity. In any discussion concerning the nature of atheism, we must remember that God has said, "For the invisible things of Him from the creation of the world are clearly seen, being understood by the things that are made, even His eternal power and Godhead, so that they [the Communists and all other atheists] are without excuse" (Romans 1:20).

Do we not have, then, a presentation of the deterioration of the mind of all who may be moving from theism to atheism? Indeed we do. The Scripture says, "Because, when they knew God, they glorified Him not as God, neither were thankful, but became vain in their imaginations, and their foolish heart was darkened. Professing themselves to be wise, they became fools, and changed the glory of the incorruptible God into an image made like to corruptible man, and to birds, and fourfooted beasts, and creeping things" (Romans 1:21-23).

The atheist, therefore, can be expected to move from sanity to depravity, from reasonable activities to abominable works. It has been well said: "If you invite an atheist over to dinner, be sure to count the silverware."

A second major feature of Marxist thought is *materialism*. This is the notion that all that exists in every possible mode of being is constructed of atoms and molecules. All is material. Materialism denies the existence of such unseen, immeasurable realities as love, honor, courage, and fidelity, yet because those concepts continue to exist in the *bourgeois* mentality, the Communists have redefined them, giving them definitions that, like their currency, are useful only within the Communist system.

Consistent materialism must even deny the uniqueness of man himself and declare that the human is merely matter in motion determined by the chemistry of his brain. The Marxists have, therefore, placed great stock in what we now call the conditioned reflex, the knee-jerk response of a mechanism to a stimulus. Pavlov's dogs were for the Communists the great lesson on the nature of the human being.

They reject the response of man to the call of his soul by describing that human activity as nonsense. World Communism has made unanswerable the question of Christ, "What shall it profit a man if he gain the whole world and lose his own soul?" In its attempt to gain the world, Marxism has left behind all matters of the spirit. What remains is the philosophic cadaver of a body without a soul.

In the place of spirit Marxism has advocated the materialism that came out of a confluence of ideas—some borrowed from the German idealist and proponent of the dialectical scheme of things, George Wilhelm Friedrich Hegel—that took place in the mind of Karl Marx. Marx called this confluence of ideas *dialectical materialism*.

For Marx, dialectical materialism referred to the notion that all of reality, and especially all historical processes, moved in a dialectical fashion. By that, he meant that a wave motion is built into the fabric of time and history. According to Marx, all societies previous to the Communist society were inherently unstable. In those societies nature itself persistently attempted to rise in successive waves of historical progress, each wave overwhelming the existing status quo. Borrowing from Hegel, the status quo Marx called the *thesis*. The opposing wave motion he called the *antithesis*. Marx claimed that it is inevitable that the antithesis overwhelm the thesis and produce a resolution of those two opposing forces called the *synthesis*.

Quickly, however, the synthesis would become the new thesis and would be opposed by the next wave, the new antithesis. With this, the same process would be repeated as the inevitable dialectic of history moved on and on.

For reasons that have yet to be explained, Marx then insisted that the last wave of history was the socialist world revolution. This wave would overwhelm the thesis—capitalist society —and bring a beautiful and lasting resolution to the forces of history. This resolution would produce the Communist utopia, the new Communist man, the final resolution of every competing force in the universe. Yes, heaven on earth would be produced by the resolution of the dialectical forces of history. For the Communist, the declaration that "Communism is the wave of the future" is not merely a slogan; it expressed the core of the Communist faith.

Marx was, however, impatient with the rate at which the forces of history appeared to be moving. For him, social evolution was not enough. Although he was a great admirer of Charles Darwin, he thought that evolution needed help from the outside. Marx's call, therefore, was for a more powerful, dynamic, forceful, world-changing form of evolution—namely, revolution. Hence his call: "Workers of the world, unite; we have nothing to lose but our chains. We have a world to win!"

A third characteristic of Marxist thought has to do with economics. It is best called *economic determinism.*

What really determines the direction in which history is to move? If there is no God, what hand of guidance is placed upon culture so that it will move inexorably toward the proper point on the compass? Marx's answer was economic determinism.

Marx believed in a form of natural selection, but he held that this selection was produced not primarily by biological forces but by economic forces. For him, the *bourgeois* societies are weak, decadent, cruel, and exploitive because the capitalists produce an economic environment that fosters these negative human qualities. Children are raised to believe that they own their clothes, their shoes, their bicycles, and later, their automobiles and homes. Marx saw this concept of personal possession as the grossest of evils because he believed that what a person presumed to own he owned in contrast to, indeed in opposition to, the good of society. To Marx the individual counted for nothing and was only significant as he functioned for the good of society. The greatest evil was that which is inimical to the advancement of the Marxist society; and the greatest good was that which advanced the Marxist society.

The good society Marx saw as only coming to pass through an economic revolution that removed all possessions from the hands of the individual and placed them into the hands of the state. Then the class struggle would disappear and everyone would work "according to his ability" and give to each "according to his need," to quote the famous dictum.

But for Marx, the guidance of mere economic determinism was not a strong enough engine to accomplish his ends. There must be a firmer hand upon the wheel of history. That firmer hand would be the god he invented—the Communist Party.

Marx saw the true Communist as a person possessed with profound insight, a limitless vision for the future, a willingness to do anything to bring that future to pass, and a total loyalty to the Party.

Instantly, as anyone can see, there was created the great contradiction to Marxism—a new class. The Communist Party instantly took to itself all possessions, all power, all ability to lead. The Party became the custodian of every plan for the future and of the life of every individual in the system. So it was that Marx, who advocated with his dying breath a classless society, created a new, firmer, crueler class than any bourgeois society in the whole world.

Yes, the Communist Party became a god. The mind of man has been so created by God so that it cannot function as an autonomous entity. It must have an ultimate truth, a final authority, a god it sees as the fountainhead of all values and from which all final truth is derived. Having denied the existence of the living and true God, Marxism in cynical contradiction turned to atheism to create a god for man to serve joyfully—the Party.

It can safely be said that all of the thousands of derivations of Marxist thought are built on these basic principles of Marxism that are at the core of Marxist thought: atheism, dialectical materialism, and economic determinism.

Now any system of philosophy that purports to change the world must over the passage of time prove its point. The test of time is the great test any philosophic view must eventually face. A thousand systems can be created in as many clever minds, and at the beginning have no need for proof. They are stated as articles of faith, even though they were in fact created in midair by people who call themselves philosophers, sociologists, historians, and ideologists. We can thank God that out of these 1,000 intellectual concepts, 999 disappear without a trace. They fall with a moan into the grave of their originators and are unheard of by subsequent generations. Most such systems are quickly and mercifully decapitated by a perceptive rebuttal in the period in which they were presented. A thoughtful public usually gives them a quick analysis and declares them to be nonsense.

Unfortunately, that did not happen with Marxism. It was a system with a sufficient voice and a wide enough constituency to override those who stood to claim of it, "Lies, all lies!"

No, Marxism gathered momentum and became a mighty force in the world. Under the leadership of Vladimir Ulich Ulanov (who changed his name to Nikolai Lenin so that he could write somewhat anonymously) it took to itself organizational structure and the fire and steel of revolution. Lenin became the organizer that Marx needed to produce the revolutionary cadres for the revolutionary conquest of *bourgeois* nations.

During the turmoil of World War I, Lenin made his play. By this time, he was one of the best-known revolutionaries in the world and was even being observed by the police forces of a number of nations. He lived at that time in Zurich, Switzerland, where he spent his days brooding over the possibility of revolution in the Soviet Union. For that matter, he would have been happy for revolution in a Communist direction in any of the nations of the world. Looking at the crumbling monster of Russia, however, he thought that it would be the best opportunity.

The Germans thought so, too. They considered that if a Bolshevik revolution could be stimulated in Russia, that would take their eastern enemy out of the war and greatly enhance their own chances of victory against France and the West. The Germans therefore became co-conspirators in the Russian Revolution.

Through their spies in Zurich, the Germans communicated with Lenin and offered him the opportunity to return to Russia. Sensing that history was laying its hand of destiny upon his shoulder, Lenin accepted. Complicated arrangements were made, and Lenin, along with his party, was moved by secret train across Germany into Russia. His arrival in St. Petersburg created a spectacular impact and was considered something of a miracle by the people. Immediately, he took to the soap box and with fiery speeches raised the call to overthrow the czar. The response in St. Petersburg by the citizenry was just enough to give success to Lenin's revolution. By the narrowest of votes by the people's representatives, Lenin seized the reins of government.

So it was that Russia, weakened by the war and dispirited with the leadership of the czars, became the first nation to be captured by "the wave of the future." Before his death in 1924, Lenin announced that the Communist conquest (revolutionary deliverance) of Russia was just the beginning. Having begun, he said, Communism would then move out across Europe, Asia, and the United States and would inevitably become the master of the world. Then government would wither away, police forces would be no longer needed, the family itself would become irrelevant, and the blessed society, the Communist utopia, would come to pass. Perfect happiness would come upon all men as the social contradictions of the world were resolved. So, bright with the promise of a changed world, there began under Lenin and then under Stalin one of the blackest eras of history.

The Communist parties of the world, encouraged by the example of Russia, moved out in their attempt at the ideological conquest of the rest of the nations. In the following years, they captured by subversion and aggression Eastern Europe, China, North Vietnam, North Korea, Cuba, Ethiopia, and other hapless nations.

They came with their promise of Communist utopia. They murdered multitudes who resisted. They also killed by the millions those who even lifted a voice in disagreement. Before the world as a whole was fully aware of what was happening, one-third of its population was captured and fell under the iron control of the Communist world dictatorship.

Virtually every day following that remarkable program of conquest, the Communists announced that they were on their way to turning the world into a virtual paradise. Yes, there would be delays and problems, but the coming of the perfect society was inevitable.

The world now has a right to ask, Have the Communists kept their promise? Have these captured nations become workers' paradises?

The answer to these questions is clear and tragic. There is now on record what the philosophy of Marx has produced in flesh and in fact. That record is a terrible one indeed. Aleksandr Solzhenitsyn had this to say of it:

I am very much aware that eastern Slavic orthodoxy, which, during the sixty-five years of Communist rule, has been subjected to persecution even fiercer and more extensive than that of early Christian times. . . .

In this persecution-filled age, it is appropriate that my own very first memory should be of Chekists in pointed caps entering St. Panteleimon's Church in Kislovodsk, interrupting the service, and crashing their way into the sanctuary in order to loot. And later, when I started going to school in Rostov-on-don—passing on my way a kilometer-long compound of the Checka-GPU and a glittering sign of the League of Militant Atheists—school children egged on by Komsomol members taunted me for accompanying my mother to the last remaining church in town and tore the cross from around my neck.

. . . Orthodox churches were stripped of their valuables. . . . Tens of thousands of churches were torn down or desecrated, leaving behind a disfigured wasteland that bore no resemblance to Russia as such. . . . People were condemned to live in this dark and mute wilderness for decades, groping their way to God. . . . 15,000,000 peasants were brought to death for the purpose of destroying our national way of life and of extirpating religion from the countryside. . . . Hatred of religion is rooted in Communism. . . . Khrushchev simultaneously rekindled the frenzied Leninist obsession with destroying religion. . . . The ruinous revolution has swallowed up some sixty million of our people.[10]

Sixty million people dead. What a story of hell on earth! Why?

Solzhenitsyn sums up the reason for these fearful developments: "Men have forgotten God."

It is fair, then, to ask the question, Is Marxism true? If the truth of a point of view is known by its fruits, by its results, the answer is obvious. Considering its dominance for so many years of Russia, China, Eastern Europe, and other nations, it can reasonably be said that Communism has been responsible for the violent, sadistic deaths of at least 100 million people. It has closed tens of thousands of churches, burning many to the ground. It has kept hundreds of millions of people in the most abject slavery known to the history of man. It has developed the prison system Solzhenitsyn described as gulag archipelago,

10. Aleksandr Solzhenitsyn, "Men Have Forgotten God," *National Review*, July 22, 1983, p. 872.

working millions of slave laborers to the point of disease and death in the cruelest slave labor camps the world has ever known. More than many books could be filled with the egregious results of the pitiful philosophy of Karl Marx. The mind gropes for words to describe the pathetic gullibility of the millions of people who became willing Communist cadres and whose lives are now the stumbling, burned-out remains of a groundless faith and a hopeless future.

Make no mistake about it, though: Marxism continues to be a powerful force in our time. There are many ways in which it continuoo to oxort a romarkablo influonoo aorooo tho world. Two of them should particularly be considered.

The first is that Marxism continues to be a powerful force ideologically. Millions of young people are being trained every day in the doctrines of Marxism/Leninism. The Communists have set up an educational system whereby this ideology is presented, analyzed, and illustrated in a thousand clever ways. It is difficult for the people of a free society to realize the near-total extent to which thought control is practiced in its most sophisticated form in the educational structure, the press, and in all other avenues of information within a Communist society. To this day, any trouble that may be faced within the Communist system is not ascribed to the fallacies of Marxism/Leninism. Rather, shortages, suffering, and political instability are blamed on the fact that Communist ideology has not been properly taught. It is held that a deficiency in application is the reason for any difficulty, rather than a shortage of truth. Communist methodology may therefore be altered, but Communist ideology retains a stubborn constancy.

The influence of Marxism must also be considered immensely strong because of the retention and expansion of the military establishment in the Soviet Union. Even in these days of *perestroika* and *glasnost,* while the West is reducing its military capability, the opposite is taking place in the Soviet Union, so much so that the President of the United States admitted reluctantly, "Yes, I am concerned about the expansion of the Soviet military machine in these very days."

All suggestions to the contrary, because the Soviet Union has retained its military capability it must be seen as not having yet abandoned its intention of world conquest. A dictatorship must be evaluated not in terms of its stated intentions but rather in terms of its retained capability. For the Marxists, stated intentions, promises, and agreements are something very different from what we in the West think them to be. For us, for the most part, an agreement is an agreement. For the Communists, it is simply another device to use in lulling its enemies into submission and causing them to mistakenly interpret Communist intentions as benign. Foolish is the nation that looks at the most powerful dictatorship that has ever appeared on the face of the earth, the Soviet Union, and says, "They do not intend to use that power." That kind of naiveté is dangerous today and could be fatal tomorrow.

It also needs to be said that Communist ideology is one of the largest exports of the Soviet Union. Marxism continues to have a profound influence upon the intellectuals of the West. In greater numbers than we are perhaps aware of, the Western academicians in France, England, Germany, the United States, Canada, and many other nations are Marxist in their thinking and teaching. They reject the idea of Judeo-Christian morality in favor of atheism. For them, democracy is a naive point of view useful only as a tool to advance the Marxist party line. Consequently, the impact of Marxism on the student mind takes place not just in the Soviet Union but in Western academia as well. To many a naive student from the effete societies of the West, the maxim "from each according to his ability to each according to his need" sounds like a plausible answer to the needs of the world.

This, in part, is the reason that virtually all of the Communist leaders of today's world were recruited not as members of the toiling masses but rather as student intellectuals. "The toiling masses" is a group in which the Communists pretend to be interested, but their great thrust is the ideological conquest of the college and university campus. There they have a mouthpiece speaking for them in the form of many of the teachers of philosophy, sociology, history, and especially journalism. Nor are the schools of religion in the West without a Marxist interpretation of religion and of Christianity in particular.

If something is too good to be true then it is probably not true. That should be kept in mind by anyone who hears of the breakdown of Marxism in the Soviet Union. The man buried beneath a tombstone at Highgate Cemetery in north London still retains influence across the world beyond what many grasp. On that tombstone are written the words "Philosophers have attempted to interpret the world, but their real purpose is to change it." That is a task the ghost of Marx is still attempting to carry out.

5
Thinking Further About Marxism

Marxism has produced the greatest degree of social, physical, and moral ruin the world has ever known. Wherein does it err?

Marxism errs in four ways. It is first of all *poor economics*. Marx preached that there were laws of economics that could not profitably be violated but if obeyed would produce a classless society and consequent utopia. He even attempted to articulate what those laws were. But in the end his arguments are unconvincing. Why is that so?

It is so because Marx's arguments lack a base in the realities of economics. In his discussions of value in *Das Kapital*, for instance, Marx asserts that the value of a given commodity can be derived by summing the cost of the raw materials and the labor invested in manufacturing the product. He discusses this point for many pages—but ignores completely the point that value is not truly derived from cost but is instead derived from utility. No matter what a thing costs to manufacture, it is valueless if no one will pay to buy it. No matter what price may be assigned a product by the manufacturer, the actual value of the product is determined only when someone puts up the cash to pay for it. Other components of value are irrelevant.

Yet to this day the Soviet Union imposes state control of prices and has a currency so lacking a connection to demand and productivity that it only works within a closed system, and even then not well. When the Russian ruble passes into a free society where there is no state mandate to use it as a medium of exchange, it becomes even more useless, losing more than 90 percent of its so-called value. So again, value is not derived from a declaration of the Party but from utility in the real world.

Marx deals at great length with the matter of value in *Das Kapital*. He would have us believe that the ultimate problems of the world derive from the fact that the *bourgeoisie* has stolen the "excess value" called profit from the *proletariat*. As a result, Marx argues, the *proletariat*, the working class, labors in utter hopelessness, drops deeper into discouragement, and finally dies in distress because of capitalist exploitation. From this come all of the difficulties the world faces, he says.

In taking this view, Marx is actually making profit a life force by which the world is run. For Darwin, the life force was natural selection, but for Marx, it is excess value. He who possesses this excess value has in his hands mastery of the world, the future, and the universe. He is escalated to a godlike level and marches across history, conquering and to conquer.

Marx saw the possession of value as the natural right of the *proletariat*. Slaves are transformed into world-changers the moment that excess value, having been taken from the capitalists, is put into their hands. Profit is the Promethean fire, the lodestone, the Holy Grail, the key to divinity. The Marxist man is the god of the future. Stupendous is the destiny that will come to the sons and daughters of the Party when the economic value stolen from them by the *bourgeoisie* becomes theirs.

What a load to put on mere economics! This is hysteria, not economics. It may even be "good hysteria," but bad economics it is.

Marxism is also *bad psychology*. It is a pure illusion to believe that millions of people are trembling with ecstasy in anticipation of the prospect of laboring "each according to his ability" so that they can give to their fellow man "each according to his need." If Marx's understanding of human attitudes is true, it is impossible to prove from any evidence from any place on the face of the earth, especially in the Soviet Union.

Russia, a very large country, has a gross national product only 25 percent that of the United States. Why is this? It is simply that the competent will not work extensively and dependably to support the incompetent. Especially are they reluctant to support a tyrannical state whose leaders live in splendid wealth and grind people into poverty.

Splendid wealth it is. How wealthy was made evident in November 1989 when East Germany deposed its Communist dictatorship.

What an event that was. On November 9, 1989, James Baker, Secretary of State for the United States, said, "Three days ago, no one in the world could have predicted this event." That day, 100,000 people had come over the Berlin Wall to West Berlin and had greeted their new freedom with ecstasy. They toasted one another with champagne, danced on top of the Berlin Wall, and greeted old friends whom they had expected never to see again in this life. It was one of the greatest outpourings of ecstasy that the world has ever seen over a given political event.

Out of all of this, the Communist government of East Germany was deposed. The astonishing part of it was that Erich Honecker, the leader of the East German state, was found to be a wealthy man indeed. The press brought the report that he owned thirty-two homes, which he used as residences at one or another time. They reported also that he imported one hundred tons of grain every year from the West in order to feed the stags at his private hunting reserve, so that he and his cronies could have good hunting.

One can imagine the revulsion felt by the people when they heard this. This hypocritical man had preached for years that the East Germans must make great sacrifices in order to bring the Communist paradise to pass in the future. Few East Germans suspected that Honecker had created his own paradise in the present.

The story was the same in other Eastern European nations. Romania was a noteworthy example. Nicolae Ceausescu, who with his wife was executed Christmas Day 1989, was also a man of great wealth. He had subjugated the Romanians in one of the most oppressive dictatorships on earth, even to the extent of killing thousands of them who would not obey his commands.

After his execution, the press carried stories about Ceausescu's wealth similar to those reported about Honecker. He had built for himself a palace bigger than the one at Versailles. When the revolutionary government opened the palace and people were conducted on tours through it, they were staggered at its splendor. So great was their astonishment that they wondered what to do with the building, wondered what use it might have in any future government.

It is now more than ever common knowledge that the Communist dictators are hypocrites. They impose great programs of austerity on their people, but they themselves live in splendor beyond the imagination of most of the inhabitants of earth. These late revelations can only increase the difficulty Communist leaders will have in calling their people to sacrifice. For such a call to succeed, it must be presented more strongly

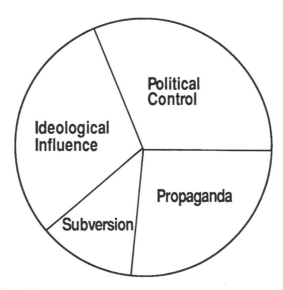

Fig. 5. Relative strength of the sources of Marxist influence

and—sad but true—a greater show of force must be used to back it up.

In addition, Communism is *bad futurism*. In any circumstance it is difficult to the point of impossible to predict the outcome of a given action. We do not know what the day or the hour shall bring forth. Still, Communism has arrogantly boasted that over time the Communist man will be produced, the state will wither away, and utopia will emerge. The Communists have been repeating this baseless boilerplate for more than a hundred years, while all the while the opposite is actually taking place. The state is not withering away, and utopia is not coming to pass. The restive masses are courageously starting to say to their leaders, "Get out and let us lead our own lives and make our own decisions."

One of the great lessons to be learned about life is that any given situation comes to pass from multiple causes and produces multiple consequences. That elementary truth escapes many foolish people who think that they can predict the exact outcome of a given individual action or group activity. No matter how genuine may be the intention and how thorough-going the preparations, the outcome of anything is, in the last analysis, unknown to us. Especially is this true when one arrogates to himself the authority to predict the outcome of group activity.

As the 1990s began, the world saw an illustration of this truth. Millions in Eastern Europe had lived behind the Iron Curtain their entire lives. According to the Communist promise of personal and social conditioning, these people could be expected to be loyal and true sons of the Party. But alas for the Communists, exactly the opposite was revealed to be true.

When the states of Eastern Europe renounced Communism, the people began coming forward with grisly stories as to what the parental state had done to them in trying to bring about the appropriate social conditioning. These people will, in all probability (we must be careful about predicting the future), be some of the most hard-boiled opponents of Communist ideology in the world. Futurism and humility go hand in hand. The Communists have never been very good at either.

A fourth shortcoming of Communism is that it is *pitiful theology*. Any system of thought that begins with the statement

"There is no God" produces instant intellectual vertigo. Having no first principle, no epistemological foundation, it cannot prove secondary assertions, tertiary thoughts, or even up, down, or around. Logic that begins in midair cannot finally demonstrate the truth or falsity of anything. The theological propositions of Communism are no more dependable than the wind in the willows. Surely the test of time proves this to all thinking people. Unfortunately, many must endure the test of time who will not early on force themselves to apply the test of logic or the test of Holy Scripture.

Admittedly, the word *theology* should be applied reluctantly to the Communist system of thought. Nevertheless, the statements the Communists have made about God, destiny, the future, human shortcomings, the object of faith, and many other things are obviously similar to theological propositions, as a comparison of Marxist propositions and the propositions of Christian theology makes evident.

The Communists assert that there is no God, whereas Christians insist that God is and that He presides above the nations.

Marxist thought denies the existence of original sin, whereas Christians know that "all have sinned and come short of the glory of God" (Romans 3:23).

The Communists insist that the conversion experience comes about because of the transport of discovering the truths of dialectical materialism. The Christian knows that being born again comes about through faith in Jesus Christ.

The Communists believe that the world changes because of revolutionary activity and continues to be viable because of the ongoing revolution against the vestiges of *bourgeois* mentality. The Christian knows what is the true wellspring of rebirth: a person becomes a new creature only when he receives Christ as personal Savior, and his continuing viability is a consequence of the wonderful promise of "Christ in you, the hope of glory" (Col. 1:27).

As for the future, the Communist has nothing to promise except an atheistic utopia, whereas the Christian knows that the future is in the hands of God. Utopia will be produced only when Christ comes again, for He only is the Lord of the universe and the One who can bring utopia to pass.

On the matter of Communism and theology, a development has taken place in our generation that has come as a surprise to those who thought about the future just a generation ago. That development is the Christian-Marxist coalescence called Liberation Theology.

It was my opportunity to attend a conference held at the Vatican in the early 1960s under the tutelage of Pope John XXIII. The motto of the conference was "Peace on Earth," and much was said about this fascinating subject.

In reading through the literature distributed at the conference, I was fascinated to notice that a new call was being extended that was unheard of in Christian theology previous to this time. The call was for a *rapprochement*, a *détente*, between Catholicism and Communism. One and another speaker talked about the possibilities of a Marxist-Christian dialogue and then of a coming together of these two hostile entities for the purposes of affecting the future.

My reaction was, *This is most interesting—but it is quite ridiculous.* No one, to my knowledge, thought of a Marxist-Christian dialogue as a serious possibility. The reason for this cynicism on the part of both the Marxist and Christian communities was that there was no rationale, no theological construct, by which such a merger could be justified or even understood.

Soon, however, that construct was invented—liberation theology. This interesting set of views grew out of Latin American Catholicism and has, as it is now reported, captured one-half of Roman Catholicism. Liberation theology has also captured the Protestant left and is not without its influence on evangelical Christianity.

What is liberation theology? It is the view that holds that Christ came into the world to be our economic liberator. It asserts that His first purpose was to free the poor and the oppressed from the shackles of economic constriction.

In actuality, liberation theology redefines sin. In liberation theology *sin* is to possess wealth in the face of the world's poverty. *Righteousness* is therefore to redistribute that wealth, giving it to the poor.

Evangelism is also redefined. It is seen as the announcement of the economic liberation of Christ and the invitation to the oppressed peoples of the world to join in the revolution He now ordains.

Liberation theology advances another fascinating rationale. In that possessing money is the essence of sin, it follows that the most sinful system in the world is capitalism. The liberationists then ask, From whence does capitalism come? The answer is, of course, the United States. For the liberationist, then, the sinful system is capitalism, the iniquitous nation is America, and the great Satan of the world is the President of the United States. Most interestingly, by these twists of logic liberation theology joins the Marxist cause and advocates the overthrow of the United States—and, for that matter, Christian civilization—in the oncoming Marxist revolution.

Absurd as this may sound, liberation theology is very strong in many parts of the world, especially in the nations of the southern tier. And although it has lost ground in some places, liberation theology continues to be a serious spiritual subversion within Christianity and a serious threat to the stability of the world. It has been called "the greatest threat that the Church has faced in all of its history."

The emergence of liberation theology makes clear that Marxism moves across the world in many a strange disguise. The predictions of its early expiration may therefore be exaggerated to an unsafe degree.

More than the remains of Karl Marx lie today in Highgate Cemetery. There also are buried the hopes, the dreams, the human possibilities of more millions of pitiable souls than the world will ever be able to imagine. But, also, the ghost of Karl Marx continues to move across the world.

Beware! It may be more than a poltergeist.

6

Closing the Book:
Julius Wellhausen

The Suicide of the West!

That is the title of a book by James Burnham we would all do well to read. It is the statement also of a condition that Burnham sees as coming to pass in our time. One of the interesting points in Burnham's book is the assertion that the West remembers enough about Christianity to feel guilty for its sins but not enough to recall where forgiveness comes from. He believes there is evidence of a profound deterioration in the most important entity on the face of the earth today, an entity the world cannot do without, the Christian religion.

There are many who now convincingly argue that the Christian religion, as it exists in the world today, is but a shadow of its once proud former self. In examining the recent past to see if this charge is really true, one is forced to consider deeply a near-death blow that came upon the church in the last century, the debilitating influence of which has remained with us until today.

From whence came this near-fatal attack on Christianity? What was its nature, and how do its results continue with us? To discover the answers to these questions, we must once again look east, in the direction of Europe. Many have been a part of the development that so changed Christianity, but none more prominent or more influential than a group that might be called "the European intellectuals."

Europe, we do well to remember, was the home of both the Reformation and the Enlightenment. Those two streams—the secular and the sacred—battled one another through the years of the previous century. They contended on many a campus and many a cloister with their alternative views of the basic questions of life.

Rousseau, with his bizarre notions about nearly everything, was often called the father of the Enlightenment. Belying this dignified title, Rousseau's ideas about the nature of man, the reason for government, and the wellsprings of human destiny became the bizarre set of contradictory notions that, as we have seen, were as responsible as anything else for producing the French Revolution.

Not only so, but the intellectual ferment of the eighteenth century set up a new climate of thought for the nineteenth century. Everything was to be questioned. The truths or the convictions of yesteryear were not to be reviewed, and even the meaning of "meaning" was the object of many new questions. In the nineteenth century, the answer to such questions as, What is man? Who is God? What is government? and, Why are we here? changed under the revolutions of that convoluted time. The revolutions also took the form of the mental, the moral, the spiritual, and in a new way the contending forces of thought involved themselves in the battle for the minds of men. As we might well expect, religion itself was not spared. This reshaping of basic concepts produced new, but not necessarily better, thinking about everything.

Until perhaps the middle of the last century, if a person in the West called himself "religious" it meant something. He would normally have been an Orthodox Protestant, an Orthodox Catholic, or an Orthodox Jew. There was a well-accepted general understanding as to what those words meant. The Bible was the authoritative book, the government was to be respected, order in society was to be kept—that's the way it was.

But that is not the way it was for long, for in the nineteenth century the view was adopted that things in this world are subject to change without notice.

One of the most fundamental of those changes was the one that occurred within that long-standing and sacred entity called the Christian religion. That change was so dramatic, so fundamental, so far-reaching that it can be said that because of it the Christian religion, though retaining its external form, became a fundamentally different thing on the inside. At the close of the century, the churches were still there, the choirs still sang, the babies were still baptized, and the candles continued to burn, but the substance, the core—yes, the life—of Christianity was gone. The idea that God was in the midst of it all and that He had revealed Himself in His inspired, infallible Word—that idea, that life, slipped through the fingers of an unsuspecting church in those days.

What happened? The answer is clear.

Religious liberalism was born. It happened in rather simple fashion. A German rationalist scholar stepped to the fore.

His name was Julius Wellhausen.

Wellhausen was an Old Testament scholar, an intellectual, and a theologian. Wellhausen became the object of great interest and produced a colossal change within the church by presenting to the Christian community a new, and he would say better, way of understanding the Bible.

Before Wellhausen came on the scene the Bible was generally accepted as the revealed, true, and inerrant Word of God. Christians everywhere believed that all of Scripture was given by inspiration of God; it was breathed by the Lord Himself and was therefore totally dependable and useful for all matters of doctrine, reproof, correction, and instruction in righteousness. In the Bible we had a book we could trust. Man's reason may be incorrect at certain points, but the Bible was infallible.

Wellhausen, along with other German rationalist theologians, turned all of that around. He held instead that human reason was totally dependable and insisted that it was the Bible that could not seriously be trusted. He presented the idea that the Bible, far from being the Word of God, was in fact a sublime collection of human documents. For instance, he insisted that we must not hold that Moses wrote the Pentateuch. Rather, this history of early man was given to us by a number of writers, whose views were compiled to form what we now call the Pentateuch. Therefore, the story of Adam and Eve is a lovely myth that can illustrate certain truths, but it surely does not represent the actual story of people whom God called "Adam" and "Eve."

Wellhausen also insisted that the subsequent account of various events given to us in the Old Testament was a product of evolutionary thinking, rather than divine inspiration. Until the advent of Wellhausen and the German rationalists, the answer to the question, Can I trust my Bible? was Yes, a thousand times yes! After that, the answer was Of course not. You can trust human reason, but certainly not the Bible, to be the sole dependable source of divine revelation.

Wellhausen presented his views to the world in *Prolegomena to the History of Israel,* calling for a new understanding of the nature of the revelation of God in the Bible. At this point, 1878, a new wind began to blow through the churches, the schools, and the homes of Germany and Europe. It was the cold wind of doubt, distrust of God, and spiritual disquiet, and it has continued to blow from then until now.

That cold wind of change was not uninfluenced by the coming of Darwinism and Marxism. But Wellhausen's book marked a decisive turning point. From that point, the advent of anti-revelational liberalism, Christianity ceased to be a religion based on *divine revelation* but rather became a set of composite religious views anchored in *human reason.* Revelation was doubted and then denied, and rationalism took its place. So fundamental was the change, and so long-standing and deadly were the results, that Wellhausen can be regarded as one of the seminal thinkers who rule the world from their graves.

Julius Wellhausen was born May 17, 1844, in Hamlen, Westphalia, Germany. Following his undergraduate studies, he gave himself to the study of theology at the University of Göttingen. His diligence as a student and his brilliance in comprehending the nature of things brought about his appointment as professor of theology at Greifswald University. His tenure at Greifswald lasted for ten years. During those years, he departed step by step and year by year from the view that the Old Testament and New Testament Scriptures came to us by divine inspiration. As a result, he was dismissed from his professorship at Greifswald. He was able, however, to continue his career in teaching theology as an extraordinary professor of Oriental languages at Halley. He later taught at Marberg until 1892, at which time he became professor in a similar post at Göttingen.

During his career as a theological professor, Wellhausen published many books in the German language on the subject of biblical criticism. Over the years, his reputation grew as the leader of a school of thought concerning a method of interpreting the Old Testament Scriptures. This school of thought came to be called *Higher Criticism*. Paul Heinisch, whose *Theology of the Old Testament* was translated into English by William G. Height, gives us insight into the thinking behind the new form of biblical interpretation of which Wellhausen was at the center: "Scholars who will not admit divine revelation seek to explain Old Testament belief in God in terms of evolution. They would have Old Testament monotheism be the resultant from lower stages, or from polytheism, or regard it as a peculiar instinct of the Semites, or as borrowed from neighboring nations."[1]

The perceptive reader will note the introduction of the ideas of Darwin on evolution into Old Testament biblical scholarship. There can be no doubt that the biological assumptions Darwin pressed upon our world were soon transposed out into the wider world of thinking on many subjects, including theology. We can learn more of Wellhausen from Heinisch.

> The Wellhausen School maintains that pre-Mosaic religion in Israel had been polydemonism in the form of totemism, animism, ancestor worship, fetishism. Recent investigations in the countries of the ancient Orient, however, have demonstrated that the religions of the Near East as far as can now be ascertained, did not sink to such levels; they were polytheistic in character (star worship, personification of natural forces), and tapered off in a monarchical system. Rather than evolution, there was retrogression, because the number of gods gradually increased. Furthermore, prehistory testifies that primitive man was in no way intellectually inferior to his descendants, and that at least in the realm

1. Paul Heinisch, *Theology of the Old Testament* (St. Paul, Minn.: Liturgical, 1955), p. 34.

of art he was quite superior. Ethnology also refutes the theory of religious evolution, for the concepts of the so-called primitive peoples are purer than those of their neighbors already engaged in agriculture and cattle raising. Therefore, we need but give scant attention to those passages which have been cited as containing traces of the above-mentioned "isms."[2]

We notice, then, that to enhance his view that the Bible is a collection of interesting documents rather than the Word of God, Wellhausen invented an account of prehistory that has been decisively refuted by later scholarship.

One other passage can be cited from Heinisch's *Theology of the Old Testament* to support this point. Under the heading of "The Notion of God's Justice Before the Period of the Literary Prophets" Heinisch said: "Belief in God's justice, i.e., that He rewards the good and punishes the wicked, dates to the most ancient ages of mankind. It was not, as claimed by the Wellhausen school, first proclaimed by the literary prophets. Our first parents were driven from paradise because they had disobeyed God's command."[3]

To understand Wellhausen's impact upon textual criticism, we need to know something of the work of his predecessors and their theories in this area, a view that came to be known as the Documentary Hypothesis of the Pentateuch. This fine-sounding phrase simply means this: at least four authors made a contribution to the first five books of Moses—that is, Moses may have been a contributor, but he did not write the entire Pentateuch.

In 1678, Richard Simon, an oratorian Catholic priest, put forth the hypothesis that the Pentateuch had at least two authors: a Yahwist and an Elohist. That was so, Simon said, because the two writers used the names Jehovah and Elohim for God in the respective portions of Scripture they wrote.

Wellhausen took this idea several steps further. His contribution was to clarify respective authorships by establishing definitive criteria and by chronicling the biblical books, dating them by a central postulate of the science of comparative religion. That postulate was the assertion that cults indigenous to

2. Ibid., p. 34.
3. Ibid., p. 86.

one another evolve in the same manner: from a plurality of gods to a unified deity. This evolution occurs roughly at the same rate, since the cults' geographic proximity provides a social, economic, political, and religious catalyst toward mutual change. From this postulate, Wellhausen concluded that those portions of Scripture that deal with sophisticated doctrine (the one God, the decalogues, the Tabernacle, and so on) may have been inserted at later dates than those passages that were simple narratives. According to Wellhausen, then, some passages, including all of Deuteronomy, were written as a result of an evolutionary process and not by divine revelation.

Wellhausen regarded Israel's history prior to the beginning of the monarchy of Israel as uncertain. Exodus, he thought, was completely historical; prior to that, all was myth.

Wellhausen's scholarship became an important contribution to liberalism as it sought to demythologize the Bible by taking God and spiritual things out of it. Through this means, Wellhausen opened the door for subsequent scholars to expand the base of liberalism and add to it their own interpretations of biblical truth. Some found the Bible to be an endless round of allegories rather than necessary historical truth.

The logical consequence of all of this speculation was a defection from sound doctrine by the church and its leadership, as well as a fundamental shift in religious allegiance from Christianity to an empty humanist religion. Although the Bible still remained, because of Wellhausen it was dry pages of variable human theory, rather than the living, breathing revelation of the eternal God.

Instead of the mosaic authorship of the Pentateuch, he presented the authors E, J, P, and D—and others. The expression "EJPD" may be familiar to the reader who remembers it as the core of the Documentary Hypothesis. The suggestion of the Wellhausen school was that the first chapter of Genesis used the name of God "Elohim." Subsequent to this, another writer used the name "Jehovah" for God. The book of Leviticus was quite obviously written by a priestly mind, and so this was known as "the Priestly document." Deuteronomy became "the D document," and so the authors of the Pentateuch were summed up under the expression "EJPD." Again, the insistent message was that anybody by the name of Moses was irrelevant, and that in these documents we have a representation of myths that teach us something about God, rather than anything that should be called divine revelation. Revelation disappeared, and reason took its place.

As a consequence, the Christian religion became a complex set of human rationalizations, rather than the revealed truth of God. This defection from the orthodox view of Scripture was the evisceration of Christianity, leaving it a mere religion, without life, without hope, without authority. The initial effect of German rationalization upon a Christian culture was on the schools, churches, and scholarship of Europe. Profoundly affected by the influence of intellectual pride, the Christian leadership of Europe in the colleges, universities, and then in the churches cooperated with the rationalist theologians and themselves became liberal. Quickly, the state churches embraced the rationalistic point of view and lost the concept of divine revelation. Along with this, they lost faith in the Bible.

Even so, religion still continued in Europe. There were still large churches, burning candles, beautiful choirs, lovely stained glass windows, congregations, and sacerdotalism—all of that was still there. What was gone was spiritual life. The Bible was only empty pages written by men who were now dead, rather than the revelation of the living God. European Christianity was destroyed from within while still possessing the external form by which it had been known for centuries. Like a formerly intelligent man who has taken leave of his senses and become jibbering and irrational, so was European Christianity. The leaders quoted everything but the Bible and preached everything but the gospel, and reality was gone.

Moreover, it was because of religious liberalism that Europe lost its soul. To this very hour, it is still in search of that soul. It can accurately be said that if Europe does not discover spiritual reality once again, if it does not turn to Christ, the Prince of Life, it may produce the prince that shall come (Daniel 9:26).

An interesting saga followed the spiritual surrender of Europe to religious liberalism. It concerns the United States and the nations of the western hemisphere.

Soon after it came into being, liberalism leaped the ocean and began to be preached in the old-line denominational churches, colleges, and seminaries of the eastern seaboard of the United States. The writings of the intellectuals of Europe argued that the new understanding of the Bible would bring a marvelous, liberating rise of humanism and deliver America from the shackles of the divine laws that were ours by revelation.

The great scholar J. Grescham Machen discussed those days and the coming of liberalism to the Methodists, the Anglicans, and ocpecially the Presbyterians. Machen reminded us in his important work *Christianity and Liberalism* what liberalism truly is. He valiantly held to the truth of the Word of God, announcing to the churches of America that liberalism was a sham. It traveled under the guise of true Christianity but was in fact an entirely different religion. It used the familiar words *God, Christ, Bible,* and *inspiration* to mean something different from what had been the traditional use of those expressions.

A word from Machen who, more than most, was conscious of the issues of those days, may be appreciated:

> In the sphere of religion, in particular, the present time is a time of conflict; the great redemptive religion which has always been known as Christianity is battling against a totally diverse type of religious belief, which is only the more destructive of the Christian faith because it makes use of traditional Christian terminology. This modern non-redemptive religion is called "modernism" or "liberalism." Both names are unsatisfactory; the latter, in particular, is question-begging. The movement designated as "liberalism" is regarded as "liberal" only by its friends; to its opponents it seems to involve a narrow ignoring of many relevant facts. And indeed the movement is so various in its manifestations that one may almost despair of finding any common name which will apply to all its forms. But manifold as are the forms in which the movement appears, the root of the movement is one; the many varieties of modern liberal religion are rooted in naturalism—that is, in the denial of any entrance of the creative power of God (as distinguished from the ordinary course of nature) in connection with the origin of Christianity. The word "naturalism" is here used in a sense somewhat different from its philosophical meaning. In this non-philosophical sense it describes with fair accuracy the real root of what is called, by what may

turn out to be a degradation of an originally noble word, "liberal" religion.[4]

A further word from Machen:

> The rise of this modern naturalistic liberalism has not come by chance, but has been occasioned by important changes which have recently taken place in the conditions of life. The past one hundred years have witnessed the beginning of a new era in human history, which may conceivably be regretted, but certainly cannot be ignored, by the most obstinate conservatism. The change is not something that lies beneath the surface and might be visible only to the discerning eye; on the contrary it forces itself upon the attention of the plain man at a hundred points.[5]

One must pray that the plain man of our time will not see himself forced upon by an alien religion that is really "neo-Christianity." Each of us, whether scholar or not, must not stand idly by and watch the destruction of our Christian faith.

Machen wrote *Christianity and Liberalism* in 1924, but for many institutions, the old-line denominations, it was too late. The arguments of liberalism had already subverted many educational establishments.

The liberal argument was relatively simple and went generally as follows:

1. We know that we are here because of an evolutionary process. The great scholar Darwin taught us this, and evolution has now become a fact of life for us all.
2. Because we know that the body of man has evolved, must we not also be aware that the brain, the mind of man, has evolved as well, moving from the simple to the complex?
3. Given that the mind of man has evolved, have not his ideas, his concepts, his understanding of things also evolved, that is, matured? (The answer for many a gullible audience, was, of course, in the affirmative.)

4. J. Gresham Machen, *Christianity and Liberalism* (New York: Macmillan, 1924), p. 2.
5. Ibid., pp. 2-3.

4. If the ideas of man have evolved, has not also our idea of God properly evolved? We used to think of God as a vindictive, judgmental, frowning ruler of the universe. Now we know Him as a God of love.

5. Because God is a God of love, we must do away with the archaic concept of original sin. Sin is not a violation of the law of an offended God. God cannot be offended. Therefore, we must see sin as lack of maturity, lack of enlightenment, lack of proper evolution on our part.

6. As a solution to the problems of mankind, then, must we not hold to salvation by education? Man does not need forgiveness and redemption; he needs enlightenment. He has a spark of divinity within him that only needs to be fanned into a new flame.

7. In the pursuit of this program of the enlightenment of man as a way of salvation, we will do away with the old, ugly activities of war, hatred, famine, and the like.

Argument along this line was convincing to many. People gathered in churches and recited, "Every day and in every way, I am getting better and better." All that was needed to transform humanity was encouragement, optimism, and thinking positively about oneself.

What mankind really needed, according to the liberals, was not the "butchershop religion" of salvation by the blood of Christ. Rather, man needed to expand his ideas and concepts about himself and his human possibilities.

Karl Marx was not without his influence in these concepts. He had preached a doctrine that was really only a form of Social Darwinism, promising the improvement of humanity if people would unselfishly sacrifice themselves for the good of the commune. Religious liberalism, therefore, developed an early alliance with the political left. Indeed, conservative Christians who had seen these tides wash upon them in Europe and in England and who now saw the same ideas taking hold in the United States described some of the great denominations of that time as nothing but Communist front organizations.

Happily, we can now look at the record and rejoice in the fact that liberalism did not win the day in the United States, carrying everything before it as it had done in Europe and to a significant extent in England. No, indeed, America had a form of frontier Christianity generally characterized by sound doctrine and an allegiance to the infallibility of Scripture. Toward the end of the last century, the preaching of Dwight L. Moody had a profound effect upon the masses of America. Before that, from colonial America forward, one and another earnest expositor of the Word of God had instructed the masses of Americans as to the essential nature of true Christianity and the inspiration of the Bible.

The result was interesting to behold. In the face of the obvious poison of oncoming liberalism, there grew up in America one of the most significant movements in the life of our nation, a movement that came to be called the fundamentalist movement. Across the East, the Midwest, and on to the Pacific, literally thousands of preachers, many of them young, began to take notice of the danger of succumbing to evolutionary, Marxist, Bible-denying liberalism. In tens, then hundreds, then thousands of churches in cities, towns, and villages across America, these earnest preachers of the Word thundered a warning against the satanic subversion of Christianity. New churches by the thousands were built, new denominations formed, and great tabernacles were attended by sometimes tens of thousands of people in the major cities of the East and the Midwest. Some of these tabernacles still stand today, their dimensions reminiscent of the concern, indeed the faith, of their builders two and three generations ago.

The tenets of faith of the fundamentalist movement were all-important to them. They preached with conviction messages centered around five points of doctrine. These were:

1. *The inerrancy of Scripture.* They believed and preached that "verbal plenary inspiration" is the way God made the Bible. A person could trust each and every word, for the Scripture cannot be broken.

2. *The deity of Christ.* In the mind of the fundamentalists, the liberals had already made blasphemous statements about the Lord Jesus, one statement even calling Him "the illegitimate son of a Jewish girl and a blonde Ger-

man Roman soldier." Such egregious liberal statements
turned the fundamentalists livid with indignation,
which found its way into their powerful preaching.
3. *The finished work of the cross.* Salvation for the fundamentalist depended upon the shed blood of Jesus Christ,
and the cross was central to everything. It was their
preaching that doubtless made "The Old Rugged Cross"
the greatest hymn of that day and perhaps of all time.
4. *Salvation by grace alone.* The fundamentalists detected
in liberalism the doctrine of salvation by works, if the
liberals preached any doctrine of salvation at all. This
was anathema to the fundamentalists, who rang the
words from their pulpit "by grace are ye saved."
5. *The premillennial return of Christ.* The doctrine of the
special mission of the church as the Body of Christ and
its deliverance from the world before the days of the
Great Tribulation that was to come upon earth—this was
the fundamentalist hope. They looked forward to "that
blessed hope and glorious appearing" of Jesus Christ,
and preached this message with fervor. Indeed, the
preaching of the prophetic Word was one of the great
strengths of fundamentalism and was almost never
heard from a liberal pulpit.

What were the results of this powerful anti-liberal tide that
moved across America? The results, of course, were that liberalism became firmly rooted in America. Its impact was largely in
the East. It was less strong in the Midwest and even less than
that in the far West. By contrast, the fundamentalist movement
grew, producing a powerful program of evangelism, a global
thrust of world missions, and a call to holy living that was of
signal influence in the United States.

It is now the case that fundamentalism has, to a great extent, been succeeded by evangelicalism. An evangelical is, as
they say, the son of a fundamentalist.

Evangelicalism unites around a strongly conservative doc-
trinal platform. It is, however, generally less willing than the
fundamentalists to take to the barricades in defense of its convictions. Within evangelicalism are elements of compromise,

some people even expressing a certain willingness to renegotiate with the liberals in order to come to a happier, more mutual understanding. Elements of evangelicalism appear also to retain sympathies with the left of the religious and political spectrums, putting what it calls "social action" virtually on a par with evangelism. Still, evangelicalism remains as a significant counterforce to liberalism.

So it can certainly be said that the rise of liberalism, its thorough conquest of Europe, and its difficulties in the United States constitute one of the most interesting religious sagas of all time. Parts of that story are yet to be told. As we near the end of the twentieth century, Europe has been racked by convulsions that are widespread in Eastern Europe, moving across the Soviet Union, and disturbing the culture more than any suspected was possible. As an onlooking world contemplates the future of Europe, it rejoices but is also somewhat disquieted. It remembers that Europe gave us the bloodiest century in the history of the world. The hills and valleys of this troubled continent are still stained with crimson from more than 50 million lives lost in two world wars and a set of related conflicts.

Why did these awful calamities come upon Europe? Could it be that, by destroying the core of its own Christianity, it committed a form of social suicide? It is obvious that Europe, despite its vaunted intellectualism, was unable to defend itself against the arguments and subversions of Nazism, Communism, fascism, the world of the occult, and other diseased ideas. External results in the life of any nation are ultimately caused by the presence or absence of a spiritual core made of divine life and spiritual blessing.

Wellhausen and his liberalism destroyed that spiritual life in Europe and nearly succeeded in the spiritual destruction of the United States. To this very day, less than 1 percent of the population of Europe is evangelical Christian. Should America descend to that point, what resources will remain to us by which we can defend ourselves against the deadly tide of our time?

No one can travel through the echoing, empty churches of Europe, and from thence to its large cemeteries without suggesting that there might be a connection between spiritual depression and the life or death of a nation. That kind of spiritual depression, coming from a Christianity that has lost the core of its spiritual reality, could yet impact with its awful consequences upon other lands that still constitute Christian civilization.

The assertion of Scripture that "blessed is the nation whose God is the Lord" is not merely a sweet, devotional remark. It is a political statement and a truth to live by. Wellhausen, having stolen from Christianity its reason for being, continues to rule from his grave. Any thinking person who looks at the origins of religious liberalism, the causes of its wide acceptance, and the fearful results that it has wrought, should certainly join the movement back to the Bible as the inspired Word of God and the Lord of history who stands behind it all, without whose blessing we cannot live.

Machen, and many hundreds of competent scholars from his day until now, have shown us that Christian liberalism is in a sense "a religion within a religion." It lives within the outer form of true Christianity, plaguing the church like an incubus. It has existed side by side with true Christianity from the time of the rationalistic subversions of the last century until now.

There is another aspect of liberalism that should continue to interest: its insistence in calling itself *Christian*. While denying the inspiration of the Bible, the deity of Christ, the virgin birth, the true nature of faith, and most of the other cardinal Christian doctrines, the liberals still want conservative Christians to think of them as "one of us." As a consequence, it is almost a rule of life that the liberals do not leave the visible church.

True even in our time, in the remaining contests (most of the early ones have been lost) between liberals and conservatives, the liberals threaten to depart and go it alone. They tell of plans to open new churches, start new seminaries, and the like. But alas, that does not happen. There is a severe strain of dishonesty about this reluctance to leave, this maintaining a pretense of Christianity by those who deny the faith. Great clarity could be wrought by the liberals if they called their religion by another name than Christianity and set up shop on their own. However, in that clarity is divine and confusion is satanic, we cannot expect this course of action by the liberals. Rather, lib-

eralism will only exist by living like a parasite off the healthy
body of the Christian church. It will draw its strength from the
concessions yet to be made by conservatives. It will labor sub-
versively until it gains a majority in an organization. Then, possessing that majority, it will move to more overt control—and
another church, another college, another denomination will be
lost forever to the enemies of the cross of Christ.

When the early church Fathers saw the advent of heresy,
they were bewildered by the behavior of those who once af-
firmed but then denied the truth. Being unable to explain this
defection on rational grounds, they ascribed heresy to a demonic
origin. For them, Satan had subverted those who once stood for
the Lord.

Their assessment of the origin of heresy is not wide of the
mark when it is applied to liberalism. The Scripture says, "Now
the Spirit speaketh expressly, that in the latter times some shall
depart from the faith, giving heed to seducing spirits, and doctrines of devils" (1 Timothy 4:1).

Defection from the faith has been a perverse tendency at all
times. The apostle Paul felt constrained to write to his beloved
brethren at Galatia, saying, "I marvel that ye are so soon removed from him that called you into the grace of Christ unto
another gospel, which is not another; but there be some that
trouble you, and would pervert the Gospel of Christ. But though
we, or an angel from heaven, preach any other gospel unto you
than that which we have preached unto you, let him be ac-
cursed" (Galatians 1:6-8).

The idea that rationalism is superior to revelation is still
with us today. The contest between these polarities grows hot-
ter, suggesting that this contest may be the final battle of human
history.

7

The Coming of
the Strange Fire

"I have just seen what hell is like."

The date was August 6, 1945. The words were expressed by an observer on a military aircraft that had just turned away from a city whose name would be printed in every subsequent history book. The event was the explosion of the first atomic bomb ever dropped over a populated area of the world. The experience of discovering what hell is like was the last remembered moment for 90,000 people whose lives were extinguished from this world in that living instant. Almost 130,000 people were killed, injured, or missing, and 90 percent of that industrial city was leveled by the bomb blast.

From that moment on, the world would never be the same again. It was at that point in time that the atomic age began as a publicly, universally recognized new era in the troubled history of mankind. The strange fire that was unleashed on Hiroshima in that fateful hour continued to burn, becoming a consideration impossible to ignore in the deliberations of presidents, kings, and parliaments until the end of time. To this very hour, the fact that we live in a nuclear age has daily conditioned the thinking of all who have anything to do with plans for peace, war, energy, manufacturing, or the safety and security of mankind. No word has attached itself more to the hopes and apprehensions of a generation than has the word "nuclear" to this generation.

Following that fateful day in August 1945, the atomic bomb was used but one more time, bringing in that devastating blast the surrender of Japan to the allied powers and the end of World War II. That was on August 9, 1945, and the grisly results were 75,000 people killed, wounded, or missing, with one third of the city of Nagasaki devastated. A stunned world looked upon these two flashes of infernal lightning and then hurried to its conference tables to think about the future. Beginning there, the nations of the world conducted trembling negotiations with one another, pressed by the conviction that "this must never happen again." All subsequent discussions about life on earth have been conducted in the shadow of that familiar mushroom cloud, out of which comes the muttering thunder that seems to say, "Never again."

Many of the events of history have been created by trends, fads, human deliberations, and the like. More often, however, the vast, world-changing tides have grown out of the mind of one person who saw what others did not see, and thought what others never thought. So it was with the nuclear era. In a sense, modern times, especially in terms of its nuclear component, have been "created" by one man.

That man was Albert Einstein.

The equations that were forged in the incomparable brain of that young man still rule the world of science. As we shall see, they still rule the world of human living as well. They have their impact upon each of us every day that we breathe air, drink water, eat food, or think about the future.

Albert Einstein was born in 1879 to Jewish parents in the city of Ulm, Germany. The definition of his profession is that he was "an American theoretical physicist," although his origins were from the continent of Europe. Surely the world ought daily to thank God that the word "American" was attached to the name of Albert Einstein. Had that word remained "German," how different the world would be today!

Einstein lived as a boy in Munich and also in Milan, and continued his studies at the Cantonal School at Aarau, Switzerland, graduating in 1900 from the Federal Institute of Technology, Zurich. In the early years of his life, his parents were concerned, for they thought him to be at best a slow learner. It seemed as if he did not have the wide, eclectic breadth of interest as did the other youthful students in his school. Therefore, their hopes were not great for this young man who seemed to take more time to think about things than appeared to be normal.

Later, Einstein testified that his slow learning ability was in fact the reason for his taking more time to think about things. He thought, however, that this did limit the subjects for which he had the time and interest to consider, and which might well have occupied, but superficially, a more capacious mind. He saw himself as a simple man and felt that his capacities were best spent in thinking more deeply about simple things. That simplicity of thought led him to probe into "the secret of the universe" more deeply than anyone of his time or perhaps of all time.

Pursuing his studies with his penetrating mind, however, he obtained his doctorate in 1905 at the University of Zurich. It was in that year that he presented to the world a scientific point of view that captured the minds of the physicists of the world and redirected the course of history.

That point of view was called "the special theory of relativity."

From 1905 onward, his reputation was firmly established and grew to the level where he was soon called "one of the greatest physicists of all time." In 1912, he accepted the chair of theoretical physics at the Federal Institute of Technology in Zurich, his alma mater. By 1913, international fame was his, and he was invited by the Prussian Academy of Science to become titular professor of physics and director of theoretical physics at the Kaiser Wilhelm Institute. In the process, he became a citizen of Switzerland, but he reassumed his German citizenship in 1914. In 1921, he received the Nobel Prize in physics for his work in theoretical physics, most notably on the photoelectric effect.

In the 1920s, Einstein continued his program of teaching and at the same time was pressed with a thousand other questions by physicists, the press, and ordinary people wherever he traveled on his public appearances. We can be very sure that through the 1920s he kept a careful eye on the growth of science, the political situation in the world, and particularly the developments on the continent of Europe. One of those developments was to effect for Einstein a change of venue and nationality. For this change all of mankind can still be grateful. That development was the rise of Hitler and the establishment of the Nazi government.

The account of those notable days is now well known across the world, political historians having analyzed them in a thousand ways. A disillusioned Germany under the Weimar Republic watched and allowed to rise to power a person and a party with stated, dreadful intentions for the future. One of the early programs of Adolf Hitler and the Nazis was the creation of an enemy in the minds of the German people. That indignation, thought the Nazis, would be an instrument to unite the German people around the Nazi promise for the future. Creating an enemy, whether false or true, is a well-known political device of every incipient dictator.

For the Nazis, that enemy was the Jewish race. There followed the Jewish pogroms, the widest persecution and largest attempt at genocide that man has known in all of history. One of the Jewish persons upon whom that persecution had a profound effect was Albert Einstein. His property was confiscated in 1934 by the Nazi government, and he himself was deprived of his German citizenship. Little did Hitler know that this single act of deprivation was to put into the hands of his future enemies the scientific know-how and the military device which would ultimately extinguish his Nazi promises and halt the war which he was to initiate. The mills of the gods grind slowly, but they grind exceeding small.

In 1933, Einstein had accepted a post at the Institute for Advanced Study at Princeton, a fortuitous move for him and for all of civilization. He therefore came to the United States in 1934 and retained his position at the Institute through the war years until 1945. In 1940, he decided to become an American citizen, which decision was ultimately to be of no small consequence in the survival of Western civilization.

We know, of course, that Einstein gave us the special theory of relativity, which gave the world a new understanding of the universe and the titanic power that works in the cosmos as a whole and in each individual, minuscule atom of that universe. From Einstein we learned that there are forces of near-infinite strength within the innocent, benign things we see every day. As an expression of these potential forces, Einstein perfected what is certainly the best-known equation in physics or mathematics.

That equation is $E = mc^2$.

The meaning of that equation is that the energy that is latent within matter is equal to the mass of that matter multiplied by the speed of light squared. Now we know that the speed of light is 186,000 miles per second. Simple mathematics would therefore lead us to understand that the explosive power within the nuclear components of any given mass is so great as to be beyond description. It was discovered that uranium was a remarkable metal, which, under proper circumstances, could be caused to release its atoms with a massive explosive force. Without exercising too strenuous an imagination, one can easily see that an entity, like a proton, which is traveling in a circle at the speed of light, is evidencing titanic energy. If that proton were released and fired in a straight line away from its circular orbit, all things in its path would be devastated. The proper combination to produce that effect was shown to the world in the blasts at Hiroshima and Nagasaki.

It is still the case that most people in the world do not understand the theory of relativity and how it was that the gigantic forces were unleashed in the nuclear bomb. Despite the inadequate knowledge of the details by the average man, however, each of us will at least note that the physicist's incursion into the world of subatomic particles has released a massivity of energy that has already staggered the imagination. The physicist sees no reason for not believing that there is enough force in a relatively small mass to blow up the entire world.

How much of this shall we attempt to understand? Einstein himself has a suggestion. He wrote:

Anyone who has ever tried to present a rather abstract scientific subject in a popular manner knows the great difficulties of such an attempt. Either he succeeds in being intelligible by concealing the core of the problem and by offering to the reader only superficial aspects or vague illusions, thus deceiving the reader by arousing in him the deceptive illusion of comprehension; or else he gives an expert account of the problem, but in such a fashion that the untrained reader is unable to follow the exposition and becomes discouraged from reading any further.

If these two categories were omitted from today's popular scientific literature, surprising little remains. But the little that is left is very valuable indeed. It is of great importance that the general public be given an opportunity to experience—consciously and intelligently—the efforts and results of scientific research. It is not sufficient that each result be taken up, elaborated, and applied by a few specialists in the field. Restricting the body of knowledge to a small group deadens the philosophic spirit of a people and leads to spiritual poverty.[1]

This was Einstein's own introduction to the good work of Lincoln Barnett in presenting *The Universe and Dr. Einstein*.

We will agree as to the wisdom of this statement by Dr. Einstein. In fact, Einstein in this passage has pointed up the difficulty faced by any author who would write on important but complicated themes (almost all important themes carry with them a degree of complication). In any form of science or in the humanities, but especially in theology, is that principle present. One fears, therefore, that in our time the popularists have achieved the clear majority. Consequently, we have much literature that is interesting but superficial. We have much literature that passes for valuable religious material or even Christian doctrine which could well be enhanced in its truth content, despite the complications.

In Einstein, we see once again how a person with a dominant, world-changing set of ideas is soon called upon to put his imprimatur on other things. Einstein, with his obviously confirmed and life-changing views called relativity, was soon to be thought the father of a set of views that were to influence the entire culture. In the minds of many, *relativity* became *relativism*.

---

1. Lincoln Barnett, *The Universe and Dr. Einstein* (New York: New American Library, 1938), p. 9.

There is no doubt that relativism is one of the prevailing thought modes of our society.

Paul Johnson, the historian, comments on this:

"At the beginning of the 1920s the belief began to circulate, for the first time at a popular level, that there were no longer any absolutes: of time and space, of good and evil, of knowledge, above all of value. Mistakenly but perhaps inevitably, relativity became confused with relativism."[2]

Einstein was chagrined at the way his presentation of physics became twisted in the public mind.

"No one was more distressed than Einstein by this public misapprehension. He was bewildered by the relentless publicity and error which his work seemed to promote."[3]

Expanding on this, Johnson said:

The emergence of Einstein as a world figure in 1919 is a striking illustration of the dual impact of great scientific innovators on mankind. They change our perception of the physical world and increase our mastery of it. But they also change our ideas. The second effect is often more radical than the first. The scientific genius impinges on humanity, for good or ill, far more than any statesman or warlord. Galileo's empiricism created the ferment of natural philosophy in the seventeenth century which adumbrated the scientific and industrial revolutions. Newtonian physics formed the framework of the eighteenth-century Enlightenment, and so helped to bring modern nationalism and revolutionary politics to birth. Darwin's notion of the survival of the fittest was a key element both in the Marxist concept of class warfare and of the racial philosophies which shaped Hitlerism. Indeed the political and social consequences of Darwinian ideas have yet to work themselves out, as we shall see. So, too, the public response to relativity was one of the principal formative influences on the course of twentieth-century history. It formed a knife, inadvertently wielded by its author, to help cut society adrift from its traditional moorings in the faith and morals of Judeo-Christian culture.[4]

2. Paul Johnson, *Modern Times* (New York: Harper & Row, 1983), p. 4.
3. Ibid.
4. Ibid., p. 5.

So it was that the popular interpreter of Einstein in his day found himself quickly saying, "All things are relative," and thinking that he was voicing a new discovery that was as true as relativity. But alas, he was speaking of an entirely different subject, which would be essentially denied by Einstein himself. Nevertheless, the notion that "all things are relative" soon moved out from the laboratory of the physicist into the entire human domain. Thus was created the era in which absolutes faded and eventually disappeared in the minds of many and in which relativism became the prevailing spirit of thought and action.

It will help in our understanding of the easy acceptance of relativism to remember the world as it was in the days of the early impact of Einstein's theory of relativity. The period of the turn of the century until the days of World War II was fascinating indeed.

As a basic background, Darwinism had taken hold with near universality. The assumption behind most teaching and virtually all related activity was that all of nature was evolving from a narrow, meaner past to a wider, better future. How easy it was, therefore, to assume that the truths, the principles, the standards, the foundations of yesterday were now irrelevant. The past, with its Victorian morality and immature concepts, was fast slipping into the shadows of yesteryear. The force called natural selection was seen to be carrying the world along—ever onward, ever upward. Nothing, then, was sacrosanct, and the belief system of man no longer held that things were changeless, secure, or absolute.

Marxism was also coming on strong not only in the Soviet Union but in other nations in the West. The world looked on with a combination of horror and fascination as the Russian Revolution swept the Marxists into absolute power. Preoccupied by the dread actualities and results of World War I, the unsuspecting nations of earth thought little of the Russian Revolution and its possible consequences. Having established itself in Russia, Marxism then easily entered the intellectual climate of the West with its call for social change and its larger ambition of global revolution.

Marx, Freud, Einstein all conveyed the same message to the 1920s: the world was not what it seemed. The senses, whose empirical perceptions shaped our ideas of time and distance, right and wrong, law and justice, and the nature of man's behavior in society, were not to be trusted. Moreover, Marxist and Freudian analysis combined to undermine, in their different ways, the highly developed sense of personal responsibility, and of duty towards a settled and objectively true moral code, which was at the centre of nineteenth-century European civilization. The impression people derived from Einstein, of a universe in which all measurements of value were relative, served to confirm this vision which both dismayed and exhilarated—of moral anarchy.[5]

Yes, the revolutionary spirit was on. Marxist cadres in Germany, France, Britain, and the United States preached their doctrines with even greater conviction and more earnest calls. Pointing to the eight days that shook the world in the Soviet Union, they promised that "this was just the beginning." They joyously extended the call of revolution to everyone everywhere and thought that in a matter of days the same bright revolution that had begun to transform the Soviet Union would come to the other nations of the world. For them, the new age of revolution had begun, and time would shortly transform everything.

The instabilities created by these moving ideas were further exacerbated by the Wellhausian destruction of historic Christianity. The evolutionary and Marxist modes came upon the churches and soon became the substitute gospel preached by the liberal religious establishment, which took the place of the message of saving faith in Jesus Christ. Very soon, the mission of the church was seen as changing the world, altering the social structure, producing social transformation. The concept that the mission of Christianity was to bring the hope of eternal life gave way to the doctrine of social action as a replacement of the "irrelevant activity" of preaching. Christianity, in the minds of its leaders, was now to be seen as the great instrument of social change, even to the place where some thought, *In our time we might bring in the kingdom.*

In the days following World War I, this was especially true. The liberal establishment announced that the awful European

5. Ibid., p. 11.

war was "the war to end all wars." They announced that mankind had learned its lesson and that dramatic changes were now
ahead with the combined forces of natural selection, Marxism,
and a new, world-oriented Christianity. The idea of change, of
moving from the old to the new, was in the air. In the midst of
this milieu of thought came relativism. It soon became fashion-
able everywhere to suggest as a universal explanation of all
things the faddish expression, "All things are relative." Here
was an assertion that had nothing to do with the science of physics or chemistry. Rather, it was a play on words, a twist of an
expression that thereby lent plausibility to those who felt constrained to use the words of the time.

So it was that at the cocktail parties, on the streets, and especially in the academic circles the relativity of Einstein developed its social application in relativism. They all insisted that
just as things were relative to one another in Einstein's universe,
so also were all relationships within the culture relative, not to
an absolute law but to an inabsolute one another. Relativism became king, and a twisted version of Einstein's views joined the
pantheon of ideas that rules from the grave.

The worst of these relativisms, of course, is moral relativism. In that the basis of life itself is moral, moral relativism
quickly moved to undermine the very foundations of society.
The ideas of "historic values" and especially "Judeo-Christian
ethics" were quickly superannuated, and all ideas of right and
wrong were suspected, reviewed, and in many cases discarded.
It can easily be argued that society began its slide into the abyss
with the advent of moral relativism and the absence of a sturdy,
rock-ribbed Church to stand as an earthwork against the tide.

But for most people, of course, complete moral relativism is
an absurdity and an impossibility. To some degree, man has the
law written in his heart and possesses, until he successfully de-
stroys it, a conscience that brings guilt to his soul, which vio-
lates that law. The fact is that the mind of the rational human
being cannot long retain its sanity in a situation where moral
guidelines have disappeared. What, then, was man to do? In that
there must be guidance of some kind, society formulated alternative ethical systems so that there would at least be some dim
light shining in the darkness. It may well be suggested that there

are four possible ethical systems to which a culture can adhere in its attempt to retain some guidance for present and oncoming generations. These four systems would well be worth noting.

The first and highest of the ethical systems available to man is, of course, what would best be called *biblical morality*. This is the conviction that God is and that He has revealed the rules by which man is required to live if civilization is to continue. Because a reminder of this ethical system may be helpful to all, it is worth a moment of review. It can probably be safely asserted that it is a rare person, even in the church, who has reviewed the law of God for civilized man in the last many years. It is found clearly presented in the Bible:

> And God spoke all these words, saying, "I am the Lord thy God, which have brought thee out of the land of Egypt, out of the house of bondage. Thou shalt have no other gods before me. Thou shalt not make unto thee any graven image, or any likeness of any thing that is in heaven above, or that is in the earth beneath, or that is in the water under the earth; thou shalt not bow down thyself to them, nor serve them; for I the Lord thy God am a jealous God, visiting the iniquity of the fathers upon the children unto the third and fourth generation of them that hate me; and showing mercy unto thousands of them that love me, and keep my commandments. Thou shalt not take the name of the Lord thy God in vain; for the Lord will not hold him guiltless that taketh His name in vain. Remember the sabbath day, to keep it holy. Six days shalt thou labor, and do all thy work; but the seventh day is the sabbath of the Lord thy God; in it thou shalt not do any work, thou, nor thy son, nor thy daughter, thy manservant, nor thy maidservant, nor thy cattle, nor thy stranger that is within thy gates; for in six days the Lord made heaven and earth, the sea, and all that in them is, and rested the seventh day; wherefore the Lord blessed the sabbath day, and hallowed it. Honor thy father and thy mother; that thy days may be long upon the land which the Lord thy God giveth thee. Thou shalt not kill. Thou shalt not commit adultery. Thou shalt not steal. Thou shalt not bear false witness against thy neighbor. Thou shalt not covet thy neighbor's house, nor his manservant, nor his maidservant, nor his ox, nor his donkey, nor any thing that is thy neighbor's. (Exodus 20:1-17)

Here we have the mandate that was placed by God upon the nation of Israel. It is the basis of civil law, without which basis no nation can long survive. It is certainly the law without which no nation can know the blessing of God. The law of God, therefore, applies to every nation on earth as the key to the one way it can please God and the one way it can know survival and sanity.

Secular society has, as we have seen, progressively ignored this law. It calls this law too tough, too religious, inapplicable, and the like. But because there must be a set of rules of some kind, the highest form of secular society has opted for another legal program by which it governs itself.

This legal program, the second ethical system, would best be called *consensus morality*. To produce this form of agreement, the leading minds within a society (what politicians were once thought to be) gather and agree together as to the mutual commitment they will make to one another. This mutual commitment then comes together with some form of writing, a constitution, a Bill of Rights, a Magna Carta, or the like. It is agreed that certain things will be legal and others will be illegal. This is followed by many hopeful statements such as, "We are not a government of men, we are a government of law." So consensus morality offers rules for conduct based on a thoughtful consensus of discerning people who meet by the light of day and determine what they shall hold to be acceptable conduct.

A set of laws based on consensus can certainly be helpful. In our time, however, we have discovered that this form of agreed-upon conduct can work only among people who are for the most part reasonable, obedient, moral—yes, lawful. If, however, the majority of the constituents of a nation become unstable, self-seeking, rebellious, unreasonable, or violent, then the consensus begins to break down. We call this form of government "democracy." We are now in the midst of discovering that democracy and its attendant laws are insufficient to control a people who become increasingly perverse.

Finally, when people decide to do what is right in their own eyes, the agreement breaks down. Democracy, therefore, can only be a temporary expedient, lasting only as long as there is within that society a majority of responsible people who have the work of the law written in their hearts. When democracy sinks to the place where it is simply an object of personal advantage by those who would exploit it to their own ends, from thence it is in great trouble. It is at the point where the concept of divine law behind democracy has been eroded and then disappears. We must recognize, therefore, that however deep a national consensus may be, it still is a free-standing arrangement. It cannot survive apart from being built on a foundation stronger than the mere statement, "We have met, and this is what we have decided." Who can doubt that most of the democratic nations in the world are even now sinking beneath the possibility of being controlled by mere organized consensus?

The third possible form of civic morality is best expressed by the word *pragmatism*. Morality becomes more personal and individualistic as private advantage moves to the fore as the rule of life. Under pragmatism, the citizens of a progressively weak nation give themselves more and more to doing the thing that is practical, advantageous, or personally profitable. They move to the conviction that whatever superficial interest they may have in others, they must, if they are to survive, look out for "number one." Such a society must inevitably become progressively atomized, with each one of its people becoming a small factor of disunity as the culture is progressively fractionalized.

We can say about pragmatism that at least it is not quite the worst of all moralities. This is due to the fact that it is sometimes very practical to cooperate, to be obedient, or to follow a rule that has been established by consensus somewhere. It is therefore possible for a society to limp along even when most of its people live for personal, rather than public, advantage.

The fourth possible form of morality, which is becoming increasingly more evident in our time, is simply called *hedonism*. Here, as in pragmatism, the individual seeks for personal advantage; but now he sinks to the place where that personal advantage takes the form of mere indulgence and personal fulfillment—yes, the lust of the flesh. In a hedonistic society, partying is the major pursuit, and alcohol and drugs and degeneracy become king. Sexual fulfillment is all there is, and all other entities cooperate to bring a false version of this fulfillment. In such a society, the popular films are X-rated and the popular talk shows center on bizarre or perverted sexual activity. Finally, there are no rules whatsoever, and homosexuality becomes merely "an alternative lifestyle" and bestiality just another form of self-realization.

Hedonism may be discussed dispassionately in a philosophy class, but in practice the passions take over. A society of hedonism is experiencing its final form of existence before it passes into a bottom-of-the-pit situation where survival is impossible. It sinks into a situation with a name that only means destruction, death, and damnation. The name of that lower form of brief existence is *anarchy*.

Anarchy, the fifth possible ethical system, is the end of the line. It is the reductio ad absurdum of moral relativism. Have we not in our time seen elements of the world culture drop into anarchy, which but for the grace of God or a quick, violent, bloody revolution means death for everyone? No perceptive person will ignore the growing evidence in our time of emergent anarchy in one or another increasingly dangerous place in our world.

Such a situation begins when some person, pretending at intelligence, says, "All things are relative." If this is true, then murder, rape, and pillage are not morally different from love, altruism, and neighborly help. The fact is that many who mouth these relativistic ideas in our time have no concept of the deep pit to which such loose talk leads. If all things are relative, then soon there is no tomorrow. Society will inevitably slip down the ladder of progressively false moralities into the pit of death and extinction. Could this be the course of our present society? Only a person characterized by incurable (and it needs to be cured) human optimism could deny that possibility.

It is fair to suggest that the world of science was enormously inspired by Einstein's theory of relativity. They saw his views as truth for the world of physics, as indeed they were. Einstein brought to the physical world a deeper truth than Newtonian physics had ever seen. This deeper, more solid truth became an enormous new force in the advancement of science. James Coleman, one of the explainers of relativity, said:

> The story behind the theory of relativity is a fascinating one which stirs the imagination more than any fiction created by man possibly could do. For here is a story of theory after theory, at first appearing successful, but disintegrating upon closer scrutiny; of

repeated attempts at surmounting insurmountable barriers, only to be met with continual dismal failure. But at last all barriers were surmounted by a superhuman endeavor which up to now has withstood all tests and attacks. This is the story of relativity.[6]

Out of these remarkable discoveries, Einstein developed an enormous respect for the universe and for the God who stood behind it all. He certainly could not be called a conventional atheist, but rather an honest Jewish theist. He was given to making such remarks as, "God is subtle, but He is not malicious." He also said the well-known, "God does not play dice with the universe." He stood in awe of the intelligent Being who, in his opinion, was behind it all.

Unfortunately, the world of external culture drew the wrong conclusions from its association with Einstein. It took to itself its own ideas of social relativism with all of the consequent results of which we have spoken. Einstein would certainly not be proud to be thought the father of the deterioration due to relativism that we have seen today.

Many will remember that the doctrine of relativism was presented in something of an "official version" of this point of view just a few years ago. It took the form of a book entitled *Situation Ethics,* written by Joseph Fletcher. This work created a bit of a stir at that time, both because of its content and because of the rather extreme illustrations Fletcher used.

One of these illustrations came in the form of a story of a woman being held by the Nazis in a concentration camp. She felt reponsible to return to her husband and children, but knew that there was only one way in which this release from the concentration camp and her return to her family could be obtained. The method was that she must become pregnant. Therefore, out of love for her husband and family, she seduced one of the guards, and in the resulting act of adultery the pregnancy was achieved. Fletcher then insisted that this was an act of higher love. It was, if you please, the committing of what the world would call "sin" in order to achieve the higher righteousness of

6. James A. Coleman, *Relativity for the Layman* (New York: New American Library, 1954), p. 6.

returning to the bosom of her family. With these and other illustrations, Fletcher attempted to prove that morality was never absolute; rather, it was "situational."

Fletcher's work, therefore, attempted to give situation ethics a degree of theological legitimacy. While this may or may not have been achieved, he did succeed in giving situation ethics a degree of notoriety.

The result of all of this is that questions such as, "What is right?" and, "What is wrong?" were discussed extensively, both in the world and also within the churches, many times these discussions coming to no conclusion. For, of course, to come to a conclusion would admit the existence of some kind of absolute. This would be thought to be rather gauche, for the intellectual fads of the time ran against it.

What was forgotten in many of those discussions is the fact that nature is a far more fixed and unchangeable thing than many were willing to admit. The influence of Darwin had caused the world to believe in a natural universe that is dynamic and emerging, one that leaves behind the old principles and forever seeks new ones. No end of mischief was wrought in the thinking of people by the Darwinist view that there is no fixed continuum that moves from the past through the present into the future. Few things could be further from the truth.

One classic illustration of this necessary point is in the form of a tide that is breaking upon us today and is called by such authors as David Noebel *the homosexual revolution*. The homosexuals would have themselves and us believe that "nature" is a permissive entity, bringing joy and fulfillment to any person practicing whatever form of sexual indulgence may appeal to him, her, or them. The homosexual simply says that his practice is "an alternative sexual preference" and feels that this short expression should answer every question and satisfy every critic.

The homosexual forgets, however, that "nature" does not allow an alternative sexual expression without exacting a precise and horrible price. One cannot, simply by making a short speech, alter the laws that God has built into nature. That is why the people of an earlier and wiser generation called such activity "perversion." Perversion it is, whatever anybody says or how many sociologists add their permission to such practices. The violation of the natural order of things is still perversion, whatever new ideas would express the hope that we should think differently.

Nature is not relative. It is unaffected by remorse, tears, love, or forgiveness, and it very seldom gives us space to repent. That's why we have human laws! The law of man may be just a bit flexible, but this is to warn us of the exactions of inflexible nature. When we approach a curve in the highway, the sign says, "Speed limit—45 miles per hour." Quite obviously, we can take the curve at 50 or perhaps 55 miles per hour. But, there is an exact instant when a car of a certain weight, traveling at a given speed, will roll out of control into the crashing finality of a ditch, culvert, or even a precipice. The good intentions of the driver, or even his philosophic views about relativism, make no difference. He is dead absolutely and buried in an absolute grave.

The homosexual revolution, by the way, is like that. Homosexuality is not only a sin against God, who may give us space to repent, but it is a sin against nature as well. With nature, there is no repentance. How many must die of AIDS before the world learns this? How many new carnages must break upon our world before mankind discovers the inflexible principle that says: "Be not deceived, God is not mocked, for whatsoever a man soweth, that shall he also reap. For he that soweth to his flesh shall of the flesh reap corruption; but he that soweth to the Spirit shall of the Spirit reap life everlasting" (Galatians 6:7-8)?

The world needs to be warned of this. The "relativistic float" in the minds of individuals by the millions and nations by the score is one of the most clear and present dangers to our society. There is coming a time when God will judge under His well-stated and exact laws every person who lives. That judgment is also promised upon a world that is in a state of near-universal moral rebellion against God. Upon that world a very non-relativistic judgment approaches.

But there is coming a day in the history of the nations that might well be called "Einstein's revenge." In it, in a sense, Einstein may have the opportunity to even the score against those who have taken the absolutism of relativity and turned it into the degeneracy of relativism. It is worth noting that there is a sense in which Einstein could be thought of as establishing his rule at the end of history and will even have a say in the way the world will end. Concerning that end, the Bible says, "But the day of the Lord will come as a thief in the night, in which the heavens shall pass away with a great noise, and the elements shall melt with fervent heat; the earth also, and the works that are in it shall be burned up" (2 Peter 3:10).

These and similar verses in the Word of God tell us of the fiery holocaust that will be the end of history for humanity, for every individual man and woman. More than often, the calamities that come upon man are a direct consequence of his rebellion from divine law. Frequently, man is himself destroyed by the Promethean fire he takes into his own bosom or uses to set ablaze the tinder-like culture in the midst of which he lives. This being the case, we should not disallow the possibility that Einstein has given to man the fire with which a foolish and rebellious generation will immolate itself. Yes, it may be that while *relativism* rules this day, *relativity* may rule tomorrow, bringing history quickly to a halt. Our world, refusing the great equation of John 3:16, may have to face the unstoppable devastation of $E = mc^2$.

We shall, however, not "officially" make Einstein one of the seven. Rather, let us remember that this truly great scientist became an unintended philosophical influence—unintended by him, that is. He influenced the world in a total sense, but he had no deliberate intent to adversely alter the presumed course of history. We shall call his influence a "background" (which it certainly was) to the twentieth century, adding a special dividend to our understanding of these times.

8

Looking Within: Sigmund Freud

"The wellsprings of the human personality!"

Those words represent the object of a quest conducted by most of the human beings who have lived in the world. Who has not, at one time or another, stopped to ask, Who am I? Why am I like I am? For many, this quest has not been a happy one, for it has led them to feel as if they are reaching into unknown passages in the dark labyrinth of the soul. The true nature of man and the shape of his spiritual being has been defined in more ways, shaped by more theories, and analyzed by more psychic approaches than probably any other entity on the face of the earth. The pursuit of answers to those questions has been infinitely complicated by the fact that few have known what they truly seek, and fewer yet have conceived of themselves as having any kind of road map by which to do the seeking.

Man has often assumed definitive knowledge of the body, for one can say a body weighs so much and is of a certain height, and one can describe it in apparently objective terms. Similarly, man has often thought that he understands his physical processes, those of the body (which, of course, he does not), but the unseen part of himself he still considers to be hiding in the world of impenetrable mystery.

That sense of the mysterious is part of the reason religious gurus, county fair fortune-tellers, nightclub hypnotists, and authoritative-sounding professors have been given so much attention by the common people of the world. In no area of thought does the common man feel more inadequate than in the area of understanding the unseen soul and undefined spirit he believes lives in himself and in others. How often have the moods, hysterias, and depressions that have emerged in the lives of people we thought we knew well brought from us the thought *I never dreamed such a thing possible.* Man is acutely conscious that there is much he does not know and that no small percentage of that unknown resides in the mysterious depths of personality. *Where shall I find out who I am?* has been the persistent question of individuals throughout history. From no known source did that answer seem to be forthcoming in any way that satisfied the questing soul.

Then it happened.

There broke upon the world the voice, the writings, and the mysterious perceptions of a man who seemed to have discovered how to define the nuances of the human psyche. Furthermore, his answers appeared to be not only scientific and scholarly, but interesting, provocative, and even titillating.

Yes, a man from the world of science touched and titillated an age such as none had done before or have done since.

Sigmund Freud was his name. Psychoanalysis was his profession, and the world, before it was done, submitted itself to his therapy. In his lifetime he had an influence both superficial and profound upon the lives of millions and upon the spirit of his age. Few people who live in Western nations have been able to escape his influence. Few, in fact, have been able to avoid the accusation of at least once thinking along the lines of this man's theory of human personality.

Sigmund Freud was born in 1856 into a most interesting family. He was the eldest son of his father, Jacob, by his father's second wife. His father had with his first wife two sons, Emmanuel and Philipp. Therefore, his mother, Amile Nathansohn

Freud, had step-sons who were as old as she. Sigmund had seven younger brothers and sisters, but had two half-brothers who were twenty years his senior. Later in life he was to consider that his network of family relationships had an effect on his personality. He was to confess that he had a lasting feeling of guilt when his younger brother Julius died in infancy, since from that point on Sigmund no longer had his brother as a rival for his mother's love.

For Freud, the faintest impressions of yesteryear were not to be discounted as influences in a person's overt thinking and covert impressions. From his later writings, we can be sure that Freud carried with him a complicated set of memories he believed was decisive in determining many of his later decisions. Memories meant more to him than to most people.

At the age of three, the young Sigmund moved with his family from Freiberg, a small town in Austrian Moravia where he was born. Economic changes were the primary factor in forcing the move, but a secondary element was the strong feeling of anti-Semitism in Freiberg, sentiment that would have created difficulties for the Freuds, who were Jewish. Later the family moved to Vienna, where Freud obtained nearly his entire education. These moves, which might easily be considered normal for a family in our time, Freud described in his autobiography as the basis of his phobia of trains and traveling. His account of his early education is significant for the pattern of life evident even then: "At the gymnasium I was at the top of my class for seven years, I enjoyed special privileges there, and was required to pass scarcely any examinations. Although we lived in very limited circumstances, my father insisted that, in my choice of a profession, I should follow my own inclinations. Neither at that time nor indeed in my later life, did I feel any particular predilection for the career of a physician."

Freud's biographers note that these school years brought to him a degree of self-confidence that was to be one of his characteristics for all of life. That self-confidence explains in part why throughout his life Freud seemed relatively uninterested in conforming, pleasing others, or fitting in and was relatively unperturbed by being thought odd or iconoclastic, which was indeed his reputation with many people.

Freud, though part of a Jewish family, never formally adopted the Jewish religion. In 1926, he wrote, "The Jews treat me as a national hero, although my contribution to the Jewish cause consists solely of the fact that I have never denied my Jewishness." Nevertheless, the idea of a personal God who intimately interacts with man was not a part of Freud's thinking.

In the process of his early education Freud developed an interest in the naturalistic side of science, preferring experiments and research in the laboratory. Nevertheless, he pursued a degree in medicine, which he received in 1881. He took three years longer than normal to complete his medical studies—not for lack of diligence, but because of his interest in related subjects that he pursued.

In 1885 he went to Paris to study under J. M. Charcot, where he spent part of a year in medical studies and practice. Then on Easter Sunday, April 25, 1886, an advertisement appeared in the Viennese newspaper *Neue Freie Presse:* "Dr. Sigmund Freud, lecturer in neurology at the University of Vienna, has returned from a six-month stay in Paris and now resides at Number 7 Rathausstrasse." The announcement represented a significant step for Freud, for he had a greater interest in theory and experimentation than he did in the actual practice of psychiatry. But financial considerations and the practical necessities of his coming marriage had forced him to conclude that he must move to an income-producing activity. So Freud opened his medical practice in the field of psychiatry.

One of Freud's early interests in his practice in neurology was the use of the drug cocaine. In a letter to his fiancée, he observed that cocaine would win its place by the side of morphium in the field of medicine and would eventually be superior to it. He thought of it as a drug to be used against depression and also indigestion. He was convinced that cocaine was potent and harmless and that it provided the answers to certain problems in psychotherapy. Then came a wave of cocaine addiction in Vienna, and Freud was accused by the medical profession and the public of having been a part of this new drug affliction.

This first encounter with controversy demonstrated a characteristic personality trait of Freud's. Throughout his life, he would stubbornly pursue the things he felt were true and workable, even though his convictions were later to ban him from classical medicine and, as some of his contemporaries suggested, from the so-called civilized world as well. All who comment on him mention that he maintained his theories with astonishing stubbornness.

The end of this first provocative stage in Freud's life came in September of 1886, when he married Martha Bernays. His life with Martha was uneventful and unruffled—a disappointment to later biographers who assumed that a man who promoted the theories he did would have something of the bizarre in his private life.

A pointed summation of the life of Freud is given to us by Gérard Lauzun in his biography.

> Freud's achievement was that he restored human nature to its original wholeness and unity. He reestablished the connections between the visible behavior and hidden components of character and attitudes. He revealed the importance and the extent of impulses whose origin is sexual; he deciphered dreams, and rediscovered in humanity's stock of symbols and legends the conflicts which subtend the life of a collectivity or an individual. With unshakable daring and determination, working completely alone at first and later surrounded by a circle of disciples, he stood firm in the face of attacks, polemics and rebuttals. In a few years, this seeker whom we have watched anxiously groping for the right path to follow, passing from physiology to neuropathology and from thence to psychopathology, acquiring at every turn a mastery which was inadequate to his needs, eager to find masters to respect, was himself to become the master, the father, and at a stroke to take on a new stature. Sigmund Freud was to disappear and the father of psychoanalysis to take his place—vituperated, mocked, admired and gradually becoming *Tel que'en lui-meme l'eternite le change:* being "changed into himself" by eternity.[1]

Freud began his medical practice in neurology at a most interesting period in European history. A wide variety of neuroses flourished at the same time the *bourgeoisie* had the money to pay for counseling and treatment. Freud had developed a prom-

1. Gérard Lauzun, *Sigmund Freud: The Man and His Theories* (Greenwich, Conn.: Fawcett, 1962), p. 27.

ising, emergent reputation in Vienna and began to be noted as a specialist in the diseases of children. He soon was put in charge of the first Institute of Pediatrics set up in Austria, and that, along with his private medical practice, moved him into a very busy round of activities. It was at this point that he moved into the use of a therapy that was to characterize what might be called the first phase of his medical practice.

That therapy was hypnosis.

He had become familiar with this interesting mental phenomenon when he studied in Paris under Charcot. There he watched the French neurologist induce hysteria in patients, cause them to recall many lost memories, cause the hysteria to cease, and do many other things under the influence of hypnotic suggestion. At the time, hypnosis was experiencing the beginning of its acceptance by some involved in neurology, although it was rejected by others. Many thought the practice delivered valuable insights, whereas others considered it unauthentic and even the activity of a charlatan.

The questions concerning hypnosis and the fact that it was still an indeterminate medical practice were of little interest to Freud. As we have noted earlier, throughout his life Freud cared but to a very small extent for the opinions of other practitioners in his field (or, for that matter, any other field). He was resolutely determined to press strongly for the medical use of hypnosis and indeed become its champion. He himself testified on behalf of hypnosis, saying, "In the first years of my activity as a physician, my principal instrument of work, apart from haphazard and unsystematic psychotherapeutic methods, was hypnotic suggestion."

He further noted:

> This implied, of course, that I abandon the treatment of organic nervous diseases; but that was of little importance. For on the one hand the prospects in the treatment of such disorders were in any case never promising, while on the other hand, in the private practice of a physician working in a large town, the quantity of such patients was nothing compared to the crowds of neurotics, whose number seemed further multiplied by the manner in which they hurried, with their troubles unsolved, from one physician to another. And apart from this, there was something posi-

tively seductive in working with hypnotism. For the first time there was a sense of having overcome one's helplessness; and it was highly flattering to enjoy the reputation of being a miracle worker. With the idea of perfecting my hypnotic technique, I made a journey to Nancy in the summer of 1889 and spent several weeks there. I witnessed the moving spectacle of the old Liébault working among the poor women and children of the laboring classes; I was a spectator of Bernheim's astonishing experiments upon his hospital patients, and I received the profoundest impression that there could be powerful mental processes which nevertheless remained hidden from the consciousness of men.[2]

It was during the early period of Freud's medical practice, as he listened to patient after patient give an account of his past life, that Freud became convinced that aberrant behavior in the present could be traced to an experience in the past, even to the experience of a very young child. Eventually he came to believe that "the cathartic method" was the great answer to neurotic behavior, a conclusion that came like a revelation to him. By *cathartic method*, Freud meant the practice of asking the patient under hypnosis to recall childhood experiences with parents, playmates, friends, and strangers and the realities about such people.

In his therapy sessions it appeared at first that behind the apparent neuroses of a patient was one or another kind of aberrant sexual practice. Many of his patients gave such clearly stated accounts of past abuse that Freud was led to believe that they had indeed been molested by a father, a mother, or another person close to them. So it was that the role of sexual factors in neuroses became the emerging reality that was the object of Freud's concentration. At the same time, others in the field and even his associates were horrified at the subject and horrified as well at the man who made it such an important factor.

It is often stated of Freud that at this point in his career it was intellectual courage alone that carried him on. He became the object of a wide disgust by the medical profession and his friend and colleague Joseph Breuer deserted him, as was to be the case with many others in his profession down through the years.

2. Ibid., p. 38.

Still, the number of Freud's patients grew. But at the same time a suspicion began to grow in his mind about the accounts his patients gave him concerning their early lives. Though Freud had concentrated with mounting interest on his patients' accounts of sexual mistreatment, he began to have doubts about what they had said. He further researched the reports and testimonies given to him by his patients and realized that most of the seductions the patients reported had, in fact, never taken place. His theory of the cause of hysteria was beginning to break down. He later wrote that four factors particularly bothered him about the theory: his continued unsuccessful attempts to bring his analysis to a conclusion, the impossibility of believing that so many fathers were sexual perverts, the definite realization that there is no "indication of reality" in the unconscious, and the absence of memories of sexual assault in serious mental illness when the personality is invaded by the unconscious.[3]

At this point Freud thought that he had failed in his work, and he even considered abandoning his quest for the well-springs of human action.

In *The History of the Psychoanalytic Movement*, Freud said of this period in his career:

> When the aetiology broke down under its own improbability and under contradiction in definitely ascertainable circumstances, the result at first was helpless bewilderment. Reality was lost from under one's feet. At that time I would gladly have given up the whole thing. Perhaps I persevered only because I had no choice and could not then begin again at anything else. In the end I told myself that one has, after all, no right to despair if one's expectations turn out to be wrong; they must simply be reexamined. If hysterical patients attribute their symptoms to imaginary traumata, this new fact merely means that they themselves have created such scenes and fantasy. As much attention must be paid to psychic reality as to practical reality.[4]

It was at this point, Freud later said, that he "stumbled upon" the *Oedipus complex*. Oedipus was a character in Greek

3. Ibid., p. 49.
4. Ibid., p. 50.

mythology. The son of Laius and Jocasta, king and queen of Thebes, Oedipus was abandoned by his parents at birth because of the prophecy of an oracle and was raised by the king at Corinth. Eventually he returned to Thebes and unwittingly killed his father and married his mother. Oedipus's story is the subject of one of Sophocles' tragedies.

Freud saw in the Oedipus story the unconscious tendency of a child to be attached to the parent of the opposite sex and hostile toward the parent of the same sex. Freud advanced the idea that the persistence of this complex into adult life results in neurotic disorders of many kinds. Sometimes the idea of the Oedipus complex is restricted to the son's attachment to his mother; the expression *Electra complex* is often used for a similar attachment of a daughter to her father.

Over time, Freud progressively abandoned the use of hypnotism, for he distrusted some of its conclusions and saw it as a weak method for psychotherapy. More and more he went to a method of free association, where the patient was invited to associate freely any initial reaction to words and phrases that were presented by the examiner. To this day, free association is strongly identified with Freudianism.

Freud continued to develop his ideas. One of the lasting influences of his thinking was the definition, almost to the point of a diagram, he gave of the human personality. Freud saw the human personality as consisting of three somewhat overlapping components. These three components he called the *id*, the *ego*, and the *superego*. In 1923, Freud's book *The Ego and the Id* appeared, in which he somewhat revised his picture of the human personality.

For Freud, the id is the repository of the elemental components of the human personality. He said:

> This is the dark, impenetrable part of our personality, and such little as we know of it we have learned by studying the elaboration of the dream and the formation of the neurotic system. That little, moreover, has a negative character and can be conveyed only in terms of a contrast with the ego. Only by means of certain similitudes can we build up any picture of the id; we call it a chaos, a cauldron of seething emotions. We examine it as being based on one side in the somatic realm and receiving from

thence the instinctive needs which find psychic expression in the id.[5]

The id is a collection of thoughts, ideas, contradictions, desires, and impressions that have remained buried in the personality. Freud thought that only the work of analysis could bring these elemental entities to a conscious level. The id is filled with remembrances of the past that, for Freud, could still give us the best clue as to reasons for psychological aberrancies. The id also contains the unconscious, the passions, the irrationalities, and the primitive elements of human nature. Even after Freud's explanation, the id is difficult to understand, but one may think of it as an unrelated collection of things, the building blocks for whatever the personality may eventually become.

Superimposed on the id, or perhaps even an upper part of the id, is the ego. The ego is the entity through which the id interacts with the outside world. It finally formulates the personality, accepting some of the emergent emanations from the id and rejecting others. We may think of the id as being the elemental person and the ego as being the personality that in the outside world is sometimes called the real person.

Above these components of the personality was another entity, the superego. The best way to describe the superego is to say that it is something like, but not quite, the conscience. The superego has something of a judgmental function over the content of the id and the activities of the ego. It brings into the consciousness the ideas of guilt or approval. Sensing these, the ego can react to the moral dictates of the superego, rebelling against them or submitting to them.

For Freud, the superego was "the heir of the Oedipus complex." Freud saw the superego as coming into existence by identifying itself either with the father or with the mother of the individual. In fact, he believed, it might imitate the personality of one or another of the parents and thereby lead the child to imitate one of his parents or even to develop a latent hostility. So it was that Freud pictured in his mind the inner being of the human, which picture has moved into the consciousness and the table talk of our present world.

5. Ibid., p. 97.

We need also to note that Freud postulated that behind these entities lay a pair of instincts that decide the nature of life itself. He named those instincts the *life instinct* and the *death instinct*. In the personality, the two instincts are in conflict with one another and produce an undifferentiating energy that feeds into the id and becomes accumulated there.

Freud asserted that the death instinct could become loaded with erotic charges and combine with the libido to express itself in sadism or masochism. In masochism the libido turns inward upon itself. In sadism the death instinct turns outward, express-ing itself in dramatic, aggressive interaction with others.

Freud also postulated that the life instinct could be charged with libido as well and have an enhancing or even a multiplying effect upon the personality.

Libido, for Freud, was the great reality. The term is proba-bly the word most identified with Freudian psychology to this day. In its simplest terms, libido is the sexual urge or, for Freud, the sexual *instinct*. So fundamental was the libido to Freudian thought that a modern dictionary, in cooperation with Freud, calls libido "psychic energy generally; the driving force behind all human action."

Here, certainly, must be one of the most extreme statements made about anything in the history of the world. It is literally the way the modern interpreter understands the influence of Freud: it is the nearest thing to pervasive in our present time.

Many see Freud's assessment of the role of sexual energy in human activity as his legacy to the world, and a clear majority would agree with him that the sexual instinct is the drive that makes everything else happen.

There is no doubt that Freud was serious about making libi-do the universal motivation for all things. In *Civilization and its Discontents*, Freud said:

> This struggle between individual and society, however, is not derived from the antagonism of the primal instincts, Eros and death, which are probably irreconcilable; it is a dissention in the camp of the libido itself, comparable to the contest between the ego and its objects for a share of the libido; and it does eventually admit to the solution in the individual, as we may hope it will

also do in the future of civilization—however gravely it may oppress the lives of individuals at the present time.[6]

From Freud we can also learn something of the attitude toward evolution and Social Darwinism that has emerged in our culture. In *Civilization and Its Discontents* Freud said:

> The analogy between the process of cultural evolution and the path of individual development may be carried further in an important respect. It can be maintained that the community, too, develops a super-ego, under whose influence cultural evolution proceeds. It would be an enticing task for an authority on human systems of culture to work out this analogy in specific cases. I will confine myself to pointing out certain striking details. The super-ego of any given epoch of civilization originates in the same way as that of an individual; it is based on the impression left behind by great leading personalities, men of outstanding force of mind, or men in whom some human tendency has developed in a usual strength and purity, often for that reason very disproportionately.[7]

At this point we have something of Freud's attitude toward the Son of God:

> In many instances, the analogy goes still further, in that during their lives, often enough, even if not always—such persons are ridiculed by others, ill used, or even cruelly done to death, just as happened with the primal father who also rose again to become a deity long after his death by violence. The most striking example of this double fate is the figure of Jesus Christ, if indeed it does not itself belong to the realm of mythology, which called it into being out of a dim memory of that primordial event.[8]

These statements clearly demonstrate Freud's capacity to translate his ideas about human personality to the societal level, for in them he seconds the notion of cultural evolution and holds that society itself has a superego and is vying for a piece of the libido.

6. Robert Maynard Hutchins, *Freud*, vol. 54 of *Great Books of the Western World* (Chicago: Encyclopedia Britannica, 1952), p. 800.
7. Ibid.
8. Ibid.

Freud was not hesitant to voice his attitude about religion, by which religion, we can safely assume, he meant the Christian religion. Individuals, Freud said, tend to become psychotic when they are frustrated and despair of the possibilities of civil revolt with society:

> Religion circumscribes these measures of choice and adaptation by urging upon everyone alike its single way of achieving happiness and guarding against pain. Its method consists in decrying the value of life and promulgating a view of the real world that is distorted like an illusion, and both of these imply preliminary intimidating influence upon intelligence. At such a cost—by the forcible imposition of mental infantilism and inducing a mass delusion—religion succeeds in saving many people from individual neurosis. But little more. There are, as we have said, many paths by which the happiness attainable for man can be reached, but none which is certain to take him to it. Nor can religion keep her promises either. When the faithful find themselves reduced in the end to speaking of God's inscrutable decree, they thereby avow that all that is left to them in their sufferings is unconditional submission as a last-remaining consolation and source of happiness. And if a man is willing to come to this, he could probably have arrived there by a shorter road.[9]

Religion of all kinds Freud therefore saw as "mental infantilism" and "mass delusion."

Reading Freud on religion, one hears in his words the source of many a modern conversation about the nature of the Christian religion and the purpose of the coming of Jesus Christ into the world. Freud, an atheist, gave every successive detractor of the value of religion a set of clever, psychological remarks through which to express contempt for God and His work. After all, psychoanalysis was the new revelation, and psychotherapy the new salvation. The pervasive influence of Freud's views on religion continues to be a significant factor in the thought life of our present society.

One cannot escape the feeling that Freud, with all his analysis of the human personality, was more simple than we think. It is arguable that he was merely attaching names to various condi-

9. Ibid., p. 776.

tions which he, on his own authority, reported to be within the human psyche. His "science," that of psychoanalysis and psychotherapy, was new to the world. Therefore, at least at the start, there was no one to say that these cryptic conditions existed and were truly represented by the names Freud attached to them. It is almost as if Freud created arbitrary delineations in his own mind and then proceeded to superimpose them on the personalities described in the reports of his interviews with patients (many of which interviews he destroyed).

It is the nature of human condition that when we hear about things we do not understand, named by words that have never before existed, we respond with gentle curiosity. Our curiosity is gentle because at this point we are not reacting with any secondary attitude such as joy, horror, or resentment, and because the issue is interesting rather than compelling. If, however, the explanations do not come, or if they come in disquisitions equally cryptic, then we move from mere curiosity into an attitude that can only be called suspicion.

Our suspicions are then normally allayed if we have respect for the person who presented the new and unprecedented assertions. We may think, *He is a medical doctor. He is highly educated. He is a deep thinker. Who am I to disagree with what he says?* Freud was all of these. Therefore, the general public treated his assertions, which they did not understand, with due deference. In fact, the general public was not the first to react against Freud or to disparage his theories. Truth to tell, the general public has not done so to this day.

In his day Freud was looked upon with a kind of fascination mixed with embarrassment—much the same reaction a mixed crowd would have watching a film on animal reproduction. The public found in Freud enlightenment and titillation. Everywhere people were suspicious that his theories were not scientific. Yet they were carried along by an agreeable titillation. *What,* they asked, *will he say next?*

Then what he said continued to be interesting. He took us from the id to the ego to the superego to the libido and to the Oedipus complex through mounting stages of psychotherapy, and did it all by interpreting our dreams. Never mind that he changed his theories quite fundamentally several times in his life. Never mind that his "data" came from unconfirmed and quite unconfirmable testimony of his privately interviewed patients. Still, Freud carried the fascination of the West and the world with him through his lifetime and even through ours.

No, indeed, the public, far from repudiating him, made him a household figure. He was not merely the father of psychoanalysis and psychotherapy, he was the father also of pop psychology. Freud suggested that when a person makes a chance, unplanned remark while speaking of something else, he gives a sudden revelation of his true attitude. That has been called a "Freudian slip." When someone's amateur adviser professes to believe in any form of sexual determinism, he is today perceived as being a part of the "Freudian school" and not some depraved outcast. The mysteries of the soul are thought to have been understood and properly described by Freud. The public has received him well.

The fact is that it was in the professional class that the cracks in the wall first and early appeared. Chiefly because they believed his to be an overemphasis on, perhaps even an addiction to, the sexual motivation, professional psychiatrists, including Eugen Bleuler, C. G. Jung, Alfred Adler, and most of the other personal associates he had, broke with him. Each had a great deal to say about Freud in their works on psychology, and each analyzed him to the point of repudiation. Although the outside world was captured by his titillating theories, the professional world of neurology was greatly divided by the man whom many thought they could not understand.

What are the continuing influences of Freud that have had a profound and subversive effect on the thinking of the present age? Even in considering such influences, we note that some may be hard to detect, so deeply are they embedded in the psyche of the present time. Yet it is obvious that Freud changed man's understanding of himself, of his nature.

Freud drew the picture of man as consisting of id, ego, and superego, pressed by libido and influenced by the life instinct and the death instinct. These concepts are interesting enough to provide matter for rumination over many years, but fascination with them has resulted in men's failing to remember essential characteristics of humanity that must not be ignored.

The first and most important, man is made in the image of God. One of the first and most primary descriptions of the nature of man is found in a statement given to us by God Himself: "And God said, 'Let us make man in our image, after our likeness; and let them have dominion over the fish of the sea, and over the fowl of the air, and over the cattle, and over all the earth, and over every creeping thing that creepeth on the earth.' So God created man in his own image, in the image of God created he him; male and female created he them" (Genesis 1:26-27). Here in the Bible is a basic truth of the universe and perhaps the truth most basic in understanding the nature of man. Profound beyond description is the assertion from the Bible that we are images of the Being who made the universe.

It is wrong, therefore, to say that man is merely a collection of psychological forces. Even worse, it is a gross insult to say that man possesses his body, and indeed his being, as a subspecies of the animals of the field. Yet Freud's view tended to suggest all of this, as he caused man to concentrate on himself to the exclusion of the Being by whose past creative power and present grace we are able to continue our existence.

In contrast to the Freudian view, the Scripture teaches that man is a tripartite being consisting of body, soul, and spirit. The body of man was created out of the dust of the ground, but the spirit of man is the entity in which is resident the very creative power of God. Freud, in his concept of the id, would cause us to believe that the id is the essential component of man and that it exists in an autonomous fashion. Freud sees man as entirely conditioned by the environment, the pressures of life, the happy opportunities that come his way, and the purely human conditions in which he lives.

The believing Christian makes no such mistake. He knows that his essential nature resembles in a thrilling sense the nature of God Himself. He also recognizes that the soul of man grows out of the interaction between body and spirit and is the sense in which man communicates to the outside world. The believer knows that man's body and soul can be possessed, in fact, by the redemptive life of God in a literal sense. Because of his faith in Jesus Christ the believer possesses the wonderful gift of the indwelling Holy Spirit—the life of God in the lives of men. He is

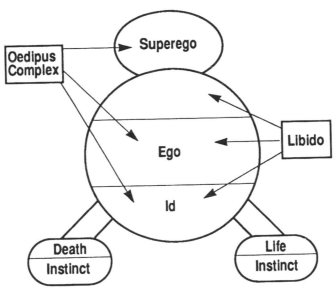

Fig. 6. The Freudian person

therefore possessed with the joy, fulfillment, and capability that come from daily contact with heaven and the sharing of the life of God. One would look in vain to the Freudian dictionary to find the marvelous assertion "Beloved now are we the sons of God."

Freudianism must inevitably lead to despair. In fact, Freud held that the death instinct finally triumphs and is the conclusion of all that matters in life. He was never known to believe in heaven or to suggest the possibility of a life to come. For him, the person of any man or any woman is simply id, ego, and superego, and all of that is soon to expire. How tragic that this despairing view should settle upon mankind. How different it might have been.

Perhaps the most critical influence Freud has upon society lies in his invention of a new determinism by which man does what he does and becomes what he becomes. Freud is interpreted as believing that libido is the prime mover, the reason that everything exists. One succeeds or fails because of his cooperation with or opposition to the forces of libido that course within his life. The notion that libido is everything is a part of the unfortunate heritage of Freudian thinking that has devolved upon mankind.

Who can doubt that the "libido is everything" philosophy has had a pervasive influence on our time? In the civilized world, up until perhaps the beginning of the twentieth century, the minds of people, at least in public, were Victorian as relates to sexual matters. For these people, still under the influence of orthodox Christianity, sexual matters were not to be spoken of. They followed the precept "Let it not once be named among you as becometh saints." The porous-minded prognosticators of our time look back on that day and call the people prudish or Puritan. They think it unfortunate that society in that day missed out on all the fun by not dragging sex into the streets, into the books and newspapers, and even into the Christian community. Yes, our present generation believes that the one who possesses morals, who possesses his vessel in sanctification and in honor, is a pitiable individual. The person who has a recalcitrant attitude toward the sexual revolution is the one who needs a psychiatrist, our pundits say.

But apart from theories about the sexual revolution, what is the record? Has it in fact been a good thing to turn our society into an open-hearth furnace of insatiable sexual activity? Who but a fool would not agree that fearful days have come upon our society because the fire—intended by God to burn within the furnace of married love—has now begun to burn across the dry and defenseless landscape?

In America, the results are clearly seen. For every two marriages there is one divorce. Although we may argue that divorce takes place for other reasons, everyone knows the real reason. The philanderers are destroying the sacred institution of marriage in America and turning the home into a temporary stopping place rather than a permanent and blessed residence.

One wonders that a society could become so gross and so stupid at the same time, believing that libido determines everything. In fact, the lack of perception concerning these things in our present society may be an indication that unbridled sex produces not only the destruction of the flesh but the deterioration of the mind as well.

The sexual revolution has also moved into the commercial society. The nearly unclothed feminine figure has become the catalyst for selling automobiles, clothing, air conditioning systems, and a hundred other unrelated items, with some to be noted but not to be mentioned.

What debilitation, what fatigue, what depression, what premature death has this produced in our society? No one will ever be able to estimate. Heaven can only suggest what marvelous individual and social advancements our world might have known had it not chosen to pour its vital, youthful energies into the sinking, sexual sands of time. What careers have been blasted, what potential melted into nothing, what great accomplishments never achieved because of our generation's incredibly nonsensical preoccupation with that never-to-be-achieved will-o'-the-wisp, that ever-unfulfilled pseudo-promise of sexual fulfillment?

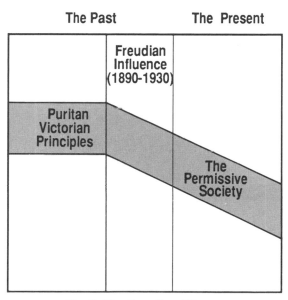

Fig. 7. The Freudian difference

The doctrine that life is significant or worthless, depending upon its sexual promise, is false. Sexual determinism is a fascinating, attractive, titillating lie.

What, then, is the determinism that makes man what he is? To answer that question, let us remember that there is moving in history a most significant force. That force is not Darwin's natural selection, Marx's economic determinism, or Freud's libido. No, indeed, that force is a prosaic-sounding entity called the will of God. Prosaic-sounding as it may be, still that is it! There is nothing else of significance in life except that—God and His perfect will for man.

What, then, is the determinism that makes life? Life is made or broken by the degree of conformity on the part of any individual or society to that knowable, divine direction, the will of God. A most profound statement is given to us in the Bible in this regard, a statement that is rarely quoted from the pew or pulpit. The apostle Paul said it well to the Corinthians: "For we can do nothing against the truth, but for the truth" (2 Corinthians 13:8).

Nothing of significance, nothing of consequence, nothing of importance, nothing that is lasting, nothing that matters can truly be accomplished which is "against the truth." All efforts in that direction are nugatory. All energy, expended in any activity whatsoever, which is at variance to the will of God is lost, never to be seen again.

By contrast, life, happiness, accomplishment, and eternal destiny are implicit in those thoughts and activities that are "for the truth." It is in that direction and for that cause that anything that is done is truly done in an intelligent sense. The key to all reality in life, to every good work that matters, is the intelligent human will responding affirmatively to the will of God.

That simple principle, if followed, will bring a thousand blessings to the perceptive soul and will save that soul from a thousand problems. It is a great mistake to reduce the motivations of life to libido or to make the wellsprings of life merely the life instinct or the death instinct. Such a conception of the potentially magnificent personality of the human individual is the grossest sort of reductionism.

More than a reductionist, Freud can certainly be called one of the great deceivers, confusing millions as to the nature of man and the nature of God. One of the great advancements for Freud is what Paul Johnson calls

> the sudden discovery of Freud's work and ideas by intellectuals and artists. As Havelock Ellis said at the time, to the Master's indignation, Freud was not a scientist but a great artist. After eighty years' experience, his methods of therapy have proved, on the whole, costly failures, more suited to cosset the unhappy than to cure the sick. We now know that many of the central ideas of psychoanalysis have no basis in biology. . . . As Sir Peter Medawar has put it, psychoanalysis is akin to Mesmerism and phrenology: it contains isolated nuggets of truth, but the general theory is false.[10]

Criticisms like this caused Freud to say that his critics were insane. "My inclination is to treat those colleagues who offer resistance exactly as we treat patients in the same situation," he said. Freud's practice has been picked up in an ominous way by the totalitarian society, Johnson says: "Two decades later, the notion of regarding dissent as a form of mental sickness, suitable for compulsory hospitalization, was to blossom in the Soviet Union into a new form of political repression."[11]

Freud also foolishly seconded the notion of cultural Darwinism. One wonders at the perverse creative imagination of an individual who invented libido for the person and then applied it to all of society. One smiles at the suggestion that society is attempting to get "a piece of that libido" in order to move enjoyably along. Nevertheless, invented by Darwin and helped along by Freud, the idea of cultural Darwinism stays with us. Out of it comes the continued assumption that there is within the ongoing culture some kind of "force," a determinism that makes it all happen.

Our present age has drawn a very foolish conclusion from this sort of thinking. Schoolbooks and advertisements on television instruct us to believe that there is something "dynamic" and "ongoing" about the world that makes it an exciting place to be. How easily we thereby succumb to the assumption that history itself possesses a force that will carry us on to progress,

10. Paul Johnson, *Modern Times* (New York: Harper & Row, 1983), p. 6.
11. Ibid.

riches, enjoyment, and perhaps utopia if we will just cooperate with that force. Yes, cultural Darwinism means nothing unless it imputes to humanity itself the possession of a life force, a cultural libido.

Many modern, cultic, and pagan religions have built their appeal on such a presumption. The modern New Age Movement insists that beings who choose to live "in harmony with nature," moving along the lines of its "life force," will discover happiness and be a part of the great utopian wave of the future. So religious have these convictions become that individuals by the thousands gather for great acts of worship in which they fall prostrate before "the sky god" and "the earth mother." They hold hands along some line, possessed by a special "magnetic resonance," and participate in a great "harmonic convergence." By harmonic convergence they mean that each one is called upon to think in unison with all of the other New Agers about a perfect world, individual fulfillment, and the utopia soon to come. The New Age Movement carries its propaganda everywhere, calling people to cooperate with the destiny they say is built into the social structure.

In giving us the determinism of libido, Freud did at least two things. First, he caused the world to concentrate on libido to the point of addiction. Second, he legitimized the creation of determinisms, thereby opening the door for the invention of the plethora of other determinisms that are being concocted in the minds of the would-be pied pipers of our time.

Freud was permitted by the Nazis to leave Austria in 1938. For years he had lived in virtual seclusion, largely because of the development of a cancer of the mouth that caused him persistent and chronic pain. He paid a ransom to be allowed to leave and went to England with his wife, his nephew, and his daughter, Anna. There he died on September 23, 1939.

Stefan Zweig gave an interesting summation of the life of Freud that will leave us thoughtful:

> This hunger of the soul for faith can find no nutriment in the harsh, the cold, the severe, the matter-of-fact sobriety of psychoanalysis. Analysis can give knowledge, and nothing more. For the very reason that it has no place for faith, it can only supply us with facts, with realities, but never with a philosophy. That is its

limitation. No other philosophical method can so successfully lead man into the recesses of his own ego; but, being an intellectual discipline and not an affective one, it can never lead him back to altitudes that transcend his own ego. It dissolves and subdivides and separates; it shows to each life its own meaning; but it is incompetent to weave the separate strands into a common meaning. If it is to be supplemented and until it becomes truly creative, the analysis and enlightenment it effects must have superadded to them a conjoining and fusing technique; psychoanalysis must be supplemented by psychosynthesis. Perhaps this will be achieved by the science of tomorrow. Freud has done marvels, but there remain other marvels still to do. Now that his art of interpretation has revealed to the mind its hidden bonds, we await the pioneers who will once more disclose to it its own freedom, showing it how to stream out of its own confines into the universe.[12]

Such a statement has New Age overtones. Such a hope can only be fulfilled by faith in the God of the universe, whose name is Jesus Christ.

12. Lauzun, p. 215.

9

The Vast Emergence: John Dewey

Have we really moved into the dawn of a new age?

That was the prevailing question throughout the Western world at the opening of the twentieth century. As the nineteenth century rolled into the twentieth, there was an all but universal sense that a new wideness, wonder, breadth of vision, and abundance of opportunities had come upon the world. All of civilization appeared to be blossoming into a fullness of flower that would make the past seem like the dark ages and the future filled with dimensions of thinking and living unanticipated by even the most happy optimists. Few of us who inhabit the years at the close of the twentieth century can sense the euphoria our forebears felt when they contemplated the future in the nascent years of "this fabulous century."

The attitude that characterized the culture of the time grew out of many streams of influence that were thought genuine and world-changing by both the thinkers and the common citizens of the West in that day—and there was some accuracy in their assessment. The streams of influence they observed were significant and world-changing. But few of those influences changed the course of history in exactly the way those living at the time thought they would.

The influences were many. During the nineteenth century, the West was moving from feudalistic attitudes and practices to the great change of culture even then called the Industrial Revolution. The steam engine, the horseless carriage, mechanized farm machinery, and machines to make machines—all seemed to be filled with bright promise. Already mechanical means had been developed that would reduce what had once been the back-breaking labor of a thousand to moderate effort of a single man operating a machine. Observing this, even the most uninspired saw in the future a day when leisure would replace labor, when contemplation would be the activity of man while the machines did the work.

That hope for an easier future made it possible for the citizens of the day to ignore the sweatshops of the major cities and other exploitations of labor that soon became common. Idealism was in vogue, and the unfortunate circumstances endured by laborers were seen as merely temporary conditions on the way to the wonderful world of the future. One of the functions of hope is to create patience, and that was the case in this instance. Hope became one of the great themes promoted by those who lived at the expense of the patience of the people they exploited.

The euphoria of the times also grew out of the fact that they were generally peaceful days. The horrors of the Civil War—which had brought about the most extensive carnage in the history of the world up to that time—were put out of mind. This still inadequately explained event was remembered largely in terms of heroism and as a great stimulant to the Industrial Revolution.

Anyone who contemplates history cannot help but notice how the gift of blessed forgetfulness is given to virtually every generation in the unrolling years of history. This gift makes it possible for a given age in the midst of its blithe optimism to repeat the fatal mistakes of a previous generation with hardly a pang of remorse or fear. So it is that successive cultures have marched to the beat of fife or drum into the red cauldron of war, pain, and death and did so by following exactly the well-worn path trod by previous young aspirants to glory.

Especially, however, the world at the turn of the twentieth century was filled with anticipation. That was because of the philosophies that had become popular. The early 1900s was the first era in which Darwin and his ideas had come to full flower. By that time, evolution was well on its way to capturing the world of academia and the thought processes of the average man. Virtually everyone believed that history was moving up from the gross and the animalistic into the sublime and even the angelic. Each individual could reasonably argue that "natural selection has selected *me!*" The natural man could think of himself as being the person on whose shoulder history had laid its hand of destiny, calling him to be a custodian of the future.

Social Darwinism was fast persuading society of a similar conviction. It claimed that no problem was unsolvable, no difficulty unresolvable. Given time enough, all would be well. Humanity had within it a potential that would not be denied. Let the naysayers and the pessimists be left behind, for nature itself had dictated progress and fulfillment, writing it large upon the bright scrolls of the future.

Of no small consequence to the development of the spirit of the times was the fact that the Christian religion, despoiled of its corrective theology, was inadequate to stem the tide of humanism. In those days, the strong and forceful preaching of the cardinal Christian doctrine of original sin would have done much. But, alas, as we have seen, Christianity had abdicated its responsibility to be a corrective within society and instead cooperated with the golden promises of the secular humanists. Moving with the tide, the church quickly changed its message of salvation through the cleansing of the blood of Christ to a message of salvation through the improvement of the social structure. Christian leaders and the great denominations saw the attitude of optimism not as a danger to society but as a godsend. The world had "finally come around to our point of view" and was thinking of human possibilities. If man is no longer a sinner, all he needs is education and inspiration, and the flame of bright possibility will burn brilliantly in all society.

That attitude on the part of the religious establishment is perhaps understandable. Although there had been significant revivals of religion in the immediate past, at the turn of the century, those revivals were not generally characterized by intellectual or theological content. Many people indeed were brought to the place where they confessed Christ, but they were brought to that place by simple preachers with a simple gospel for the common people. Out of the era immediately preceding the turn of the century there came earnest faith but not a broadly understood Christian view of God and the world. The ranks of the common people came to the point of conversion, but few were the influences of those revivals on the world of academia.

Consequently, to this day the great missing element in Western thinking is the Christian viewpoint. Western man thinks about economics, politics, government, education, and a thousand other things without ever once asking, *What has God said about these things?* The absence of the forceful pressing of that question turned the early promise of the twentieth century into the greatest series of disasters the world has ever known. It brought upon the world the greatest intellectual confusion, moral myopia, and carnage that has been seen in the history of man. We hardly need to be reminded that science without God, so vaunted in that day, can now put on one airplane more explosive power than has been expended in all of the wars in the history of mankind.

Let us also remind ourselves that the ideas of Karl Marx were gaining currency at the turn of the century. In the very wind was the promise of new philosophies, new thinking, new futures, and perhaps even an entirely new social structure to contain it all. Very quickly these ideas took hold in the West, American culture included, and then spread throughout the whole world.

How was this set of ideas able to gain so much credibility so easily? In earlier eras, emergent concepts took a long time to gain ascendancy. How was it that liberalism, humanism, and the new fluid way of thinking was able to move so far so soon? The answer will be startling to some:

These new ideas captured the American educational system.

Put another way, the complex set of new ideas, thoughts, notions, philosophies, and ways of thinking moved into what was then the world's greatest instrument for the dissemination of ideas, the public school system of America.

How did that happen?

As always, of course, there were multiple causes. However, one particular individual, an educator, was more than anyone else responsible for the transformation of the methods and the content of education in America.

His name was John Dewey.

This man, described by biographers and commentators as "America's foremost philosopher and educator," refashioned the educational system in America, moving it from the so-called static concepts of the past into a wholly new era in education. In the process, he redefined almost everything—from the nature of truth to the responsibilities of the teacher and the capacity of the human personality. His influence became pervasive in America and had an effect as well on the way students in most other nations were educated.

The influence of the man and his ideas extended through a fifty-year period during which he exercised his capacities as an organizer, prolific writer, and seminal thinker. He became a primary influence in the world of thought. That the "new thinking" at the turn of the twentieth century became "the way the world thinks" can be laid at the feet of this man who more than all others made education in America what it is today.

In the sense of history, the facts of this man's life are relatively unexciting. He did not appear as a Promethean personality, he did not fight in a great war, and he held no high political office. But, alas, he was a notable contender in the battle that matters—the battle of ideas. He was one of the prime movers in the struggle for the minds of men.

In this regard, we must remind ourselves that the essential battle of the world is exactly that, a battle for the minds of men. The struggles that matter today and tomorrow are not fought with submarines, bombers, missiles, and moving armies. Those machines of visible conflict are but the final *reductio ad absurdum* of the unseen conflicts brewed earlier in the imaginations of people that later boiled up into external, empirical reality. Millions who have perished in the nameless battles of history and who are now buried in unmarked graves died because someone failed at intellectual and moral persuasion.

The opening salvos of any war are the public announcement that the earlier spiritual, intellectual, and mental battle has been lost. John Dewey was one of history's chief contenders in that earlier, vital battle—the battle for the mind. But, alas, he was on the wrong side of that battle.

Dewey was born in 1859 in Burlington, Vermont. From his earliest youth, he was a bookish individual, a shy young man never thought of as being a brilliant student. He enrolled in the University of Vermont in 1875. As a college student he had no clear idea as to what he would pursue as a career, though during the final years of his university experience he became interested in philosophy, with a special turn toward social thought. From the very beginning of his philosophical thinking, he did not conceive of philosophy from a classical point of view. As it is normally taught, philosophy deals with the great questions of life and then teaches that an answer to those questions is embraced by one school of thought or another. For Dewey, however, philosophy was not to be so simply categorized. Rather, he saw man as living in the midst of a swirling set of ideas, issues, concerns, and problems, which set was ever changing. Those problems needed, therefore, to be considered, categorized, and then constantly reconsidered in the light of ever new, ever changing developments. Nothing must be thought of as final, settled, certainly not as foundational.

In his university experience Dewey discovered Hegel. The influence of Hegel on Dewey was initially in the area of idealism. It is interesting to note that Hegel was a profound influence upon many who were later to follow him philosophically, including Marx, Kierkegaard, and others who were to become influential in a later age. Hegel is not to be discounted as one of the prime movers of Western thought.

Dewey later testified that Hegel satisfied an intellectual craving. Dewey derived from Hegel a sense of the ideal and also the view that reality was not a fixed, hard, foundational, never-to-be-changed thing. Dewey came to see reality as change, emergence, and development, rather than as a static and fixed thing that is foundational and unalterable.

One of the most obvious characteristics of Dewey's philosophy—and one that makes him difficult to read—is the fluid nature of his views. More than often, Dewey discomfited his intellectual opponents by denying a given proposition and then refusing to affirm the opposite of that proposition, denying that as well. For Dewey, reality was something in between, but was not even permanently that. So again, truth was not to be found in static propositions but in the confirming reality of social fulfillment.

As a consequence, it has been difficult for normal Aristotilian thinkers to finally categorize John Dewey and his views. He was a philosopher but not the father of any philosophic school of thought. He was an educator but not one who saw education as the communication of some kind of final truth. He was an educational administrator but one who kept his eye persistently on outcomes rather than mechanics. Consequently, words such as *provisional, experiment,* and *unpredictability* are often applied to his thinking and his methods. The frustration of attempting to categorize Dewey is compounded by the fact that in the large number of books, essays, and magazines he wrote over the course of his life he dealt with topics in such a fashion that he could be quoted on either side of most of the current arguments. For him, nothing was constant, given, or finally true, but rather all things were pragmatic, adaptable, and subject to whatever reinterpretation seemed appropriate for the day and the hour.

The early John Dewey was certainly involved in specifics as he taught classics, science, and algebra on a high school level in Oil City, Pennsylvania, from 1879 to 1881 before returning to Vermont, where he continued to teach. Dewey then applied to the graduate program at Johns Hopkins University. Interestingly, he was refused the aid of a fellowship and was therefore constrained to borrow five hundred dollars from an aunt to begin his career as a professional teacher and philosopher. The university soon became one of the most exciting centers of scholarly and intellectual activity, and Dewey was an active participant in it all. He took the doctorate at Johns Hopkins in 1884, presenting as his thesis a dissertation on the psychology of Immanuel Kant.

That same year, at the urging of one of his former professors, George Sylvester Morris, an exponent of neo-Hegelianism, Dewey assumed a professorship at the University of Michigan. At Michigan Dewey became increasingly dissatisfied with speculative philosophy and tried to make philosophy applicable and directly relevant to the practical affairs of men. There also his economic, political, and social views became increasingly radical. His first book, *Psychology,* was followed by *Applied Psychology* in 1889.

In 1894, he moved to Illinois and became chairman of the Department of Philosophy, Psychology, and Education at the University of Chicago. His experience at the University of Chicago gave him the opportunity to consolidate his diverse interests in psychological, social, and intellectual matters. He took part in social welfare activities to a high degree, participating in the life of Hull House in Chicago, founded by Jane Addams. There he involved himself in the economic and social problems of a major urban area, interacting with the population at every level and further strengthening his conviction that philosophy must be applied to life. Also, he founded the Laboratory School, which then became known as The Dewey School, and wrote a number of important books on education, among them *The School and Society* and *The Child and the Curriculum.*

As a result of his work in Chicago, he was invited in 1904 to assume the chair of education at Columbia University in New York. From this position of influence, he labored until his retirement in 1930, gaining international prominence for his radical views in education and philosophy. The Columbia Teachers' College soon became a training center for teachers from around the world, thereby spreading Dewey's educational philosophy literally to the ends of the earth.

Dewey was instumental in founding *The Journal of Philosophy,* which became an international forum for the discussion of his ideas. From the time of its founding until Dewey's death, scarcely a volume of this journal did not contain an article either written by Dewey himself or containing a discussion of the details of his philosophy.

New York was then as now the journalistic and media center of the nation. This gave Dewey the opportunity to press his political and social views in the magazines and related publications that came from that important nerve center. He regularly wrote for such magazines as *The New Republic* and began to travel and lecture, thereby extending his influence in many places.

He lectured in Tokyo, Peking, and Nanking from 1919 to 1921 and advocated his doctrines in *Reconstruction and Philosophy,* written in 1920 and based on a series of lectures he had presented at the Imperial University of Japan. His lecture travels also took him to Turkey, Russia, and Mexico, where at many an educational center he advanced his ideas, which were considered a part of the radical ethos of the time.

So extensive were his writings over his lifetime that M. H. Thomas's bibliography of Dewey's works is more than 150 pages long. So diverse were Dewey's writings that his influence made a high impact not only in the field of education but also in virtually every other field that was a subject of intellectual inquiry. *The Encyclopedia of Philosophy* says:

> The wide effects of his teaching did not depend upon the superficial aspects of its presentation, for Dewey was not a brilliant lecturer or essayist, although he could be extremely eloquent. His writings are frequently turgid, obscure, and lacking in stylistic brilliance. But more than any other American of his time, Dewey expressed the deepest hopes and aspirations of his fellow man. Whether dealing with a technical philosophical issue or some concrete injustice, he displayed a rare combination of acuteness, good sense, imagination, and wit.[1]

So it was that as the consequence of his persistent presentation of his ideas on the lecture circuit and in printed page, Dewey was soon thought of as the man of all knowledge, the supreme intellect who could give us guidance on the subjects relevant to the modern mind. For years Dewey was the most respected educator in the world, a reputation he sustained through the unceasing output of his ideas presented to an admiring world via the printed page.

How shall we understand John Dewey?

1. *The Encyclopedia of Philosophy* (New York: Macmillan; Free Press: 1967), p. 381.

The best way to do that is to note what the man himself said about the subjects and issues that are relevant to us. Although it is true that many have despaired of truly understanding Dewey's many-faceted mind, Dewey presented some of his ideas quite candidly. He revealed, for instance, his lack of confidence in eternal truth. The highest word he used for that concept was the word *philosophy*. He said: "As for myself, then, the discussion is approached with the antecedent idea that philosophy, like politics, literature, and the plastic arts, is itself a phenomenon of human culture. Its connection with social history, with civilization is intrinsic. . . . Philosophers are a part of history, caught in its movement; creators perhaps in some measure of its future, but also assuredly creatures of its past."[2]

In this fashion, Dewey again and again neglects or refuses to admit that there is a final, unchangeable truth in the form of God and His Word. "Meaning is wider in scope as well as more precious in value than is truth, and philosophy is occupied with meaning rather than with truth."[3]

Then he hedged just a bit but restated the same conviction, saying:

> Making such a statement is dangerous; it is easily misconceived to signify the truth is of no great importance under any circumstances; while the fact is that the truth is so infinitely important when it is important at all, namely, in records of events and descriptions of existences, that we extend its claims to regions where it has no justification. But even as respects truths, meaning is the wider category; truths are but one class of meanings, namely, those in which a claim to verifiability by their consequences is an intrinsic part of their meaning.[4]

Although much can be said about this statement, it is quintessential Deweyian logic to suggest that the verifiability in truth resides in consequences.

That is why Dewey is commonly called an instrumentalist. To him education and all other activities are to be evaluated not

2. Joseph Ratner, *John Dewey's Philosophy* (New York: Modern Library, 1939), pp. 245-46.
3. Ibid., p. 247.
4. Ibid.

by their truth content (for what is that?) but rather by their consequences in the experience of the recipient of that education. So it is that Dewey cryptically said, "The ultimate problem of production is the production of human beings."

Dewey resented any tendency to produce final formulations of truth in the form he described as *dogma*, a word he used frequently.

A great tragedy of the present situation may turn out to be that those most conscious of present evils and of the need of a thorough-going change in the socio-economic system will trust to some short-cut way out, like the method of civil war and violence. Instead of relying upon the constant application of all socially available resources of knowledge and continuous inquiry, they may rely upon the frozen intelligence of some past thinker, sect and party cult, frozen because arrested into a dogma. That "intelligence," when frozen in dogmatic social philosophies, themselves the fruit of arrested philosophies of history, generates a vicious circle of blind oscillation, as tragically exemplified by the present state of the world.[5]

What then is the answer to the present state of the world?

But an immense difference divides the *planned* society from a *continuously planning* society. The former requires fixed blueprints imposed from above and therefore involving reliance upon physical and psychological force to secure conformity to them. The latter means the release of intelligence through the widest form of cooperative give-and-take. The attempt to *plan* social organization and association without the freest possible play of intelligence contradicts the very idea of *social* planning. For the latter is an operative method of activity, not a predetermined set of final "truths."[6] (Italics his)

When one considers Dewey, he must face the fact that the absence of a concept of final truth left behind Dewey a trail of ambiguity. In fact, Dewey himself said, "Although I have raised large questions, it is not my ambition to answer them."[7] Consis-

5. Ibid., p. 431.
6. Ibid., p. 432.
7. Ibid., p. 488.

tent with this confession, the world came away from its association with Dewey with that same impression. Writing on many subjects, he raised questions of many kinds. The concrete answers to those questions were frustratingly absent. The analysts of this man certainly must have felt that Dewey was a question-raiser rather than an answer-giver.

Nevertheless, Dewey continued to speak—endlessly it seems—about what must be done in every area of life, particularly the educational system. His attitude toward the moving wave of education was well expressed: "The educational system must move one way or another, either backward to the intellectual and moral standards of a pre-scientific age or forward to ever greater utilization of scientific method in the development of the possibilities of growing, expanding experience. I have but endeavored to point out some of the conditions which must be satisfactorily fulfilled if education takes the latter course."[8] Of course, Dewey's vote was for the latter course. He loved to contrast the prescientific age and the present age of the scientific method. As to the latter, he enjoyed applying to it such words as *possibilities, growing, expanding,* and especially *experience.* In fact, if it were necessary to describe Dewey's educational philosophy in a single word, that word would be the word *experience.* His methodology for the fulfillment of the philosophy of education he espoused is frequently called "the experimental method."

Dewey's position was that the educational system of his day was inadequate, a failure, and needed to be revamped. "It is time to take stock and to consider why and how the existing educational system has failed to meet the needs of the present and the imminent future."[9] His answer was typical as well.

> Part of the reason is found in the educational tradition itself. Elementary schooling was everywhere in the past devoted to the promotion of literacy. It was identified with acquiring skill in reading, writing, and figuring. Our ancestors would have been possessed of uncanny insight and imagination if they had thought of the purpose of the common school in any other than traditional terms. Higher education was almost equally controlled by con-

8. Ibid., p. 681.
9. Ibid., p. 683.

cern for symbols, namely, advanced mathematics and foreign languages.[10]

We may here gain an insight into an attitude of Dewey that has certainly influenced modern education. In time past, foreign languages and advanced mathematics were indeed considered the core of education. They came close to being thought of as absolute knowledge, contact with which would equip the student to deal effectively with the knowledge that would come to him subsequently in the educational process. Schools were expected to prooont tho focto to the students and then show respect for the conclusions the students drew from those facts. Dewey, on the other hand, appeared to be disposed toward moving quickly to the conclusions apart from the facts, in the sense of data having been built into the mind of the student. More and more attention was placed on making the student adept at participation in the democratic process as opposed to making him conversant with "three R's."

He was further critical of the past and its traditional teaching methods: "The traditional notion of 'discipline' was developed under these circumstances. The little red schoolhouse of our ancestors was a struggle of wits and often of mean strength between pupils and teachers."[11]

He declared: "There is only one way out of the existing educational confusion and drift. That way is the definite substitution of a social purpose, controlling methods of teaching and discipline and materials of study, for the traditional individualistic aim."[12]

He therefore declared: "Schools do have a role—and an important one—in *production* of social change"[13] (italics his). He declared that change was a constant in society and that anyone who did not recognize this point was under "a self-imposed hallucination." Therefore, educational methodology and content must change—constantly—to keep up with the constant and us-

10. Ibid., p. 684.
11. Ibid., p. 689.
12. Ibid., p. 688.
13. Ibid., p. 692.

ually unpredictable flow of social attitudes. He was critical of those who "as a rule opposed the studies called modern and the methods called progressive."[14]

What was the attitude of John Dewey toward religion? He gave us a revealing look at the measure of his soul in this regard, observing that

> science has the same spiritual import as supernaturalism; that democracy translates into the same religious attitude as did feudalism; that it is only a matter of slight changes of phraseology, a development of old symbolisms into new shades of meaning— such beliefs testify to that torpor of imagination which is the uniform effect of dogmatic belief. The reconstruction of the Church is a matter which concerns, indeed, the whole community so far as its outcome is concerned; while the responsibility for its initiation belongs primarily to those within the churches. The burden of conducting the development, the reconstruction, of other educational agencies belongs, however, primarily to the community as a whole. With respect to this intellectual aspect, its philosophy, it belongs especially to those who, having become conscious in some degree of the modern ideas of nature, of man and society, are best able to forecast the direction which social changes are taking. It is lucidity, sincerity, and the sense of reality which demand that, until the non-supernatural view is more completely elaborated in all its implications and is more completely in possession of the machinery of education, the schools shall keep hands off and shall do as little as possible.
>
> We need, however, to accept the responsibilities of living in an age marked by the greatest intellectual readjustment history records.[15]

What can Dewey mean except that he rejoices in "the greatest intellectual readjustment history records," a readjustment in which society and education moved from the supernatural to the nonsupernatural?

Dewey sounds for all the world as though he was advocating a crusade to foster the movement of culture in that nonsupernatural direction. "Bearing the losses and inconveniences of our time as best we may, it is the part of men to labor persistently

14. Ibid., p. 693.
15. Ibid., p. 705.

and patiently for the clarification and development of the positive creed of life implicit in democracy and in science, and to work for the transformation of all practical instrumentalities of education until they are in harmony with these ideas."[16] In this call to arms, Dewey came close to calling the presence of religion a "social faction."[17]

But we cannot help but include a further statement by Dewey that will be helpful in our understanding of his attitude toward religion. He spoke quite categorically, saying:

> But of one thing I am quite sure: our ordinary opinions about the rise and falling off of religion are highly conventional, based mostly upon the acceptance of a standard of religion which is the product of just those things in historic religions which are ceasing to be credible. So far as education is concerned, those who believe in religion as a natural expression of human experience must devote themselves to the development of the ideas of life which lie implicit and are still new science and are still newer democracy. They must interest themselves in the transformation of those institutions which still bear the dogmatic and the feudal stamp (and which do not?) till they are in accord with these ideas. In performing this service, it is their business to do what they can to prevent all public educational agencies from being employed in ways which inevitably impede the recognition of the spiritual import of science and democracy, and hence of the type of religion which will be the fine flower of the modern spirit's achievement.[18]

Here we have quintessential liberalism. The religion that must be fostered is the spiritual import of science and democracy. That is the religion that will produce the fine flower of the modern spirit's achievement.

We can see, therefore, that Dewey was near utopian in his attitude about the progress of history. He believed that the best way progress could be achieved was by influencing the content of education in that direction. He was convinced as well that he himself occupied the best pulpit in the world from which to

16. Ibid., p. 706.
17. Ibid., p. 707.
18. Ibid., p. 715.

preach the message of progress and its great promise for the future.

This being the case, we do well to attempt a summary of the ideas of Dewey, which will help in our evaluation of the nature of his influence.

1. *Final truth is illusory.* We live in a world that is ever changing, and therefore what we think of as principles are inevitably subject to alteration on a constant basis. Nothing is *planned,* but everything is *being planned.* Life is essentially process, and the only constant of which we can be sure is the constancy of change.

In this cardinal principle of his, Dewey stood against the epistemologists of the past who held to any concept of eternal truth. However, Dewey would not resist them but rather would simply suggest that their point of view should be respected but not become transcendent. In all of this, Dewey denied what C. S. Lewis called "the doctrine of objective value." Lewis, in *The Abolition of Man,* argued that when we deny the doctrine of objective value, we must as an inevitable result finally produce the destruction of humanity.

Dewey even sounds at times as if he believes that all reality is within the mind of the observer. Beauty is simply in the eye of the beholder. Nothing, therefore, is objectively true or valuable, but it is only so as it intersects some human concern.

Even while thinking of these things, we must not forget that the mind of man is teleologically oriented and must have purpose and reason. It cannot live with the endless pursuit of ever-changing values without ever coming to final conclusions. We must not doubt, therefore, that Deweyian thinking could be one of the reasons for the strange bewilderments, indeed the insanities, that have come upon our time. It is often said of Dewey's philosophy that it begins with people and ends with people—a conclusion that pleased Dewey. The trouble is, beginning and ending with people is circular thinking nowhere anchored in final truth.

2. *We must not think of truth but must concern ourselves with meaning.* Truth is a boxy, dogmatic thing with hard corners and offenses attached to it by the dogmatists. Meaning, there-

fore, is the thing because it is "the facts" interacting with the tide of the moment.

Such a line of thought gives the reader of Dewey intellectual vertigo, for *meaning* is an ambiguous and arbitrary concept lacking the universality of *truth*. Effective communication slips away when a word or concept can only be defined in terms of "what it *means* to you" and "what it *means* to me."

Now it is likely that in his classroom experience Dewey enjoyed the discussions precipitated by his ideas. Similarly, in interacting with the larger world he could only have been delighted with the endless consternation his ambiguities produced in the minds of his readers. Teachers and students everywhere read the writings of "the great man," who was reputed to have the most spacious mind in the world. Many professed to understand him, but of course, they were instantly in an argument with other persons who also professed to understand him but who had come to completely opposite conclusions regarding his ideas. The word *meaning* may sound like a sublime way to define truth, but actually it is another way to settle in, to bring upon ourselves the fog of misunderstanding and incomprehension.

3. *Truth is resident in experience.* The truth of simple syllogisms that are contemplated by the mind but unrealized in experience is to be denied. Experience, sparked by interest-creating teachers and rewarded by a sense of realization, is what education is all about.

Dewey, therefore, inveighed against the lecture method, whereby the mind of the teacher simply communicates with the mind of the student. Dewey regarded the lecture method as an inferior method of teaching. To him, truth does not consist in words, propositions, or assertions that can be communicated by language alone. Rather, he held that we cannot claim to understand anything until we have experienced it.

With this view of the ontological nature of experience Dewey opened the door to the subversion of every field of life—including religion—by existentialism. Over the years, the spirit of the age, influenced by the doctrine that truth is experience, has come more and more to entertain notions that would have been thought absurd in the past. How soon under the influence of the emotionalists, therefore, did society decide that happiness, fulfillment, the thrill, even the anticipation were more to be desired than uncolorful propositional dogma?

The doctrine that truth is equivalent to experience raises a number of questions. What kind of experience? one might ask. Do not experiences differ with each person, with each situation, with each state of mind, and with the same person, depending on his variant moods? In truth, valid experience is so varied so as to lead to the conclusion that experience, in any practical sense, cannot be defined at all. The cessation of straight thinking and the beginning of emotional questing takes place when the doctrine takes hold that "truth equals experience." Have we not, in fact, come to live in the most unsettled, the most questing world that ever has been?

4. *Teaching fundamentally depends upon experiment.* The teacher must not think of himself or herself as possessing the final methodology, and of course, not the final truth. "Give it a try and see what happens" is the motto of the day.

Now there is a grain of truth in an idea such as this. In the sciences, experiments are set up precisely to detect and evaluate the outcome of a given new combination of elements. Scientists themselves admit that science is hardly the exact thing its popular reputation would have it be.

The dangerous element in Dewey's experimentalism is that he was experimenting on human beings. The educational system he produced is a cocoon your children and mine attend in order to be the object of testing emergent educational ideas and new "studies" in this and that. It has ceased to be a place children attend to learn objective truths so that in turn they can think and act wisely and responsibly tomorrow. To Dewey, we can only discover what is the truth for today and the experiment that will be attempted tomorrow.

There are grave consequences to this view that reach down to our time. The schools of our land have, to a significant degree, become laboratories where social theories, scientific views, and educational hypotheses are tested in the lives of our young people.

This has been the case in many ways. One illustration that comes to mind is busing. Hundreds of millions of dollars have been spent transporting young people at great cost from one end of a city (and county) to another. All of this in order to achieve some arbitrary percentage of young people of one and another race in a given school, which percentage came down by fiat from a sociologist somewhere. In this exercise schools are not being thought of as educational institutions at all. Rather they are being thought of as places in which to test someone's theory as to the best way to change attitudes, outlooks, convictions, prejudices, and the like. Though the experiment is fascinating to the sociological dilettante, it is not a stimulant to education.

5. The *"Idea of God"* has meaning to those who believe. *Religion, however, must be reformed to serve mankind.* All must be instrumentalized for the sake of democracy and freedom. We must stay with a generalized meaning of the idea of God so that that generalization can take a needed shape at a given time. The idea of God is a serviceable doctrine that can be applied to one situation or another, provided it does not get too specific.

When speaking about any form of religion, Dewey again and again inveighed against religion's hardening itself into dogma. Being dogmatic about anything was anathema to Dewey. Especially was this true with regard to anything having to do with religion. Now Dewey was not unsympathetic to the teaching of religion, even Christianity, in the schools. But when he was asked the question, "What Christianity?" he decried the fact that Christianity had taken the form of various dogmas embraced by the denominations and was therefore no longer the generalized religion that could properly and profitably be presented to students in the public schools.

Dewey's generalized idea about religion, however, is most interesting. To Dewey, God as a unifying force between the ideal and the actual was the kind of supernaturalism that really mattered. He said:

> What one person and one group accomplish becomes the standing ground and the starting point of those who succeed them. When the vital factors in this natural process are generally acknowledged in emotion, thought, and action, the process will be both accelerated and purified through elimination of that irrelevant element that culminates in the idea of the supernatural.

When the vital factors attain the religious force that has been drafted into supernatural religions, the resulting reenforcement will be incalculable.

These considerations may be applied to the idea of God, or, to avoid misleading conceptions, to the idea of the divine. The idea is, as I have said, one of ideal possibilities unified through imaginative realization and projection. But this idea of God, or of the divine, is also connected with all the natural forces and conditions—including man and human association—that promote the growth of the ideal and that further its realization. . . . In this active relation between ideal and actual to which I would give the name "God," I would not insist that the name must be given. There are those who hold that the associations of the term with the supernatural are so numerous and close that any use of the word "God" is sure to give rise to misconception and be taken as a concession to traditional ideas.

In a distracted age, the need for such an idea is urgent. It can unify interests and energies now dispersed; it can direct action and generate the heat of emotion and the light of intelligence. Whether one gives the name "God" to this union, operative in thought and action, is a matter for individual decision. But the function of such a working union of the ideal and actual seems to mean to be identical with the force that has in fact been attached to the conception of God in all of the religions that have a spiritual content; and a clear idea of that function seems to me urgently needed at this present time.[19]

The perpetrators of the New Age movement would utter a hearty "amen" to such views.

This, then, is a brief look at the complex man who was John Dewey. He was a positivist in nearly every respect—except in the case of dogmatic religion, such as fundamentalism—and therefore could find a place in his cosmology for most of the current ideas, especially those that were new or emergent. He presided over what could best be called "the vast emergence" of ideas that broke upon the twentieth century like a flood and were soon to move into the conduits of the American educational system.

19. Ibid., p. 710.

What has been the result of this tide of influence that, by way of the educational system of the West, found its way into American thought?

Consideration of this question has turned into one of the most animated discussions of our time and over the last fifty years has been the object of great affirmation and great consternation. A thousand books have been written concerning what education is, what its content should be, and where it appears to be taking us now. One of the most popular of the recent analyses of modern education goes under a title with a touch of finality: *The Closing of the American Mind, by Alan Bloom.* The subject and point of view of this perceptive study by a teacher/scholar is revealed in the subtitle of the book: *How Education Has Failed Democracy and Impoverished the Soul of Today's Students.*

Bloom contrasts the "old view" of education, which provided a fundamental basis of unity that moved above class, race, religion, and national origin and that was bathed in the light of natural rights, with what is taking place today, saying:

> The recent education of openness has rejected all that. It pays no attention to natural rights or the historical origins of our regime, which are now thought to have been essentially flawed and regressive. It is progressive and forward-looking. It does not demand fundamental agreement or the abandonment of old or new beliefs in favor of the natural ones. It is open to all kinds of men, all kinds of life-styles, all ideologies. There is no enemy other than the man who is not open to everything. But when there are no shared goals or visions of public good, is the social contract any longer possible?[20]

Bloom then decries the deterioration of our schools, particularly as it applies to the solid content of education. Morals have faded and are now being replaced by a feeble attempt at creating "values." The old concepts of honor, honesty, virtue, and other truths we once thought to be self-evident are fading fast. They are either left unreplaced or are being replaced by cheap imitations such as pragmatism or profit.

20. Alan Bloom, *The Closing of the American Mind* (New York: Simon & Schuster, 1987), p. 27.

Bloom's somber view of American education is echoed by others whose writings have become virtually a tide of indignation against the failures of the American school system. In his book *Peril and Promise* newsman John Chancellor has this to say:

> If the United States runs out of scientists and engineers by the turn of the century, who will replace them? Today's thirteen-year-olds? Hardly. The Department of Education in 1989 helped fund a study of the mathematics and science skills of thirteen-year-olds in several countries. The American children came in dead last, with lower scores than the Spanish, British, Irish, Canadian, and South Korean children. South Korean thirteen-year-olds were first. The comparison was devastating. South Korea is a developing country, nearly destroyed by war in the 1950's, with a population that was mainly poor farmers a few decades ago. The United States is an economic giant, but is suffering from a softening of the brain. The Council on Competitiveness estimates that sixty thousand mathematics and science teachers in our high schools are not fully qualified to do their jobs.[21]

As if that weren't enough, Chancellor reports:

> In 1989, the Secretary of Education, Lauro F. Cavazos, reported that since 1985, American high school students had flat or declining scores on college entrance examinations and an unchanged dropout rate. One out of every four high school students does not finish school—close to one million young people. Another fourth —another million—who are graduated are functionally illiterate when they get their diplomas. Half the eighteen-year-olds in this country today have failed to master basic language, mathematics, and analytical skills. A million dropouts here, a million functional illiterates there, *every year.*[22] (Italics his)

These attitudes by modern commentators must not be thought of as isolated prejudices by those who want to be disagreeable. Phyllis Schlafley reports that thousands of parents have been deeply offended by the experience of their children in public schools. In *Child Abuse in the Schools*, she reports on

21. John Chancellor, *Peril and Promise* (New York: Harper & Row, 1990), p. 47.
22. Ibid., p. 49.

this disgust with the public school system, leading one to conclude that there is broad discontent with increasingly expensive and decreasingly productive American education.

This attitude toward the public schools is not actually a modern development. Perceptive individuals have seen the dangers of "progressive education" since the days of its introduction. The Greek scholar and theologian J. Gresham Machen, whose writings were the object of most profitable study by many of us in our seminary years, had much to say also about public education. His views should not be ignored by this generation. In *Christianity and Liberalism* (a book everyone should read) Machen says:

> When one considers what the public schools of America in many places already are—their materialism, their discouragement of any sustained intellectual effort, their encouragement of the dangerous pseudo-scientific fads of experimental psychology—one can only be appalled by the thought of a commonwealth in which there is no escape from such a soul-killing system. But the principle of such laws (the laws that require a public school education and that, at that time, were also being used to deny the formation of Christian schools) and their ultimate tendency are far worse than the immediate results. A public school system, in itself, is indeed of enormous benefit to the race. But it is of benefit only if it is kept healthy at every moment by the absolutely free possibility of the competition of private schools. A public-school system, if it means the providing of free education for those who desire it, is a noteworthy and beneficial achievement of modern times; but when once it becomes monopolistic it is the most perfect instrument of tyranny which has yet been devised. Freedom of thought in the Middle Ages was combatted by the Inquisition, but the modern method is far more effective. Place the lives of children in their formative years, despite the convictions of their parents, under the ultimate control of experts appointed by the State, force them to attend schools where the higher aspirations of humanity are crushed out, and where the mind is filled with the materialism of the day, and it is difficult to see how even the remnants of liberty can subsist. Such a tyranny, supported as it is by a perverse technique used as the instrument in destroying human souls, is certainly far more dangerous than the crude tyrannies of the past, which despite their weapons of fire and sword, permitted thought at least to be free.

The truth is that the materialistic paternalism of the present day, if allowed to go on unchecked, will rapidly make of America one huge "Main Street," where spiritual adventure will be discouraged and democracy will be regarded as consisting in the reduction of all mankind to the proportions of the narrowest and least gifted of the citizens.[23]

In this important book, Machen pours out his concern for the future of education in America and for freedom itself. Machen's book was written in 1924. What would this man say if he were to observe the schools of present-day America and the thought life of its citizens?

Our present time has brought a mounting set of concerns.

We are warned again and again of the amazing rise in the economic power of Japan and the mounting potential of Western Europe, along with the remarkable changes in other nations of the world. Virtually every analysis of the future, after speaking of the growing possibilities in Asia, on the continent, and even in the Soviet Union, refers to the decline of the United States and North America. We are indeed experiencing an increasing and staggering public and private debt, a precipitant rise in the rate of crime, a drug war (which we are losing), a rise in suicides, and a regular reminder of the awful onslaught of the AIDS epidemic. Along with these frightening statistics comes the report of the mounting cost of our school system and the declining results in the education and inspiration of our young people. The question emerges as to whether the next generation of young people will be adequate to the task of handling the growing and near unsolvable problems that are coming upon Western society.

The decline of the West—here is one of the obvious facts of life in these days. From whence comes the problem? Whose fault is it? The source may be found by first answering the question, What is the major influence upon our society, and wherein has that influence failed? The answer to the first part of that question is that the major influence upon the life of Americans in this century has been its well-developed, fully organized, ex-

23. J. Gresham Machen, *Christianity and Liberalism* (New York: Macmillan, 1924), pp. 13-15.

pensively financed educational system. The opportunity for education from kindergarten to a graduate degree is more widely available in America than in any other nation on earth. Thousands of students from virtually every nation of the world come to the United States to avail themselves of the educational resources present here, particularly training in the sciences.

At the same time, education in the humanities has faltered. The teaching of philosophy, sociology, and history has enjoyed less and less popularity. Why is this the case? Could it be that these "soft subjects" have been progressively emptied of their educational and spiritual content?

It is in the study of philosophy that the questions of final authority are considered. In medicine, the final authority is the simple issue of life and death (with a recent addition of financial capability). In science, the absolute is the speed of light, and this has now moved beyond discussion. In philosophy, however, final authority has been lost, with devastating results.

In the past in philosophy, whatever conclusions the philosopher reached, he had to begin with some doctrine of objective value. The first objective value, out of which all philosophy was built, was the existence of God. "God is!" was step A for the study of anything philosophical. Then the assumption that God was replaced with "natural law," which, it could be argued, is the next best thing. In this century, even that has slipped away.

Dewey was certainly the strongest voice advocating a circular philosophy that began with man and ended with man and that paid little attention to the old values in the process of making that circle. This anthropocentrism, this humanism, of which Dewey was a fountainhead in this century, became pervasive in our American schools, especially at the graduate level. From that point on, the ruling point of view in American education was that there was to be no ruling point of view. It was Dewey who articulated the concept best of all.

What, then, is the fault of American education? Much could be said about many things—teaching methods, money, buildings, urbanization—but behind it all is the loss of the objective value of God and His Word. When the Bible and the knowledge of God was set aside with hardly a wisp of objection, it was easy for alternatives to fill that place. Evolution, Marxism, higher criticism, Freudianism, and other alien views moved into our school system and became basic assumptions. Nor did they have to shoot their way into the pantheon of American education. No, indeed, they were welcomed as the long-sought new answers to the basic questions of life. The new gods of the mind found themselves on the platform of an auditorium to which they had been denied even admission yesterday.

Is there a chance for a recovery of the American mind? Can the educational system that so surely creates that mind yet be preserved? The hour is late. We may indeed be approaching the night in which no man can work.

While a thousand suggestions could be made as to the location of the path to recovery, one is obvious and imperative. America must return to the God of its fathers. The West must again become in truth a "Christian civilization." It must recover the doctrine of objective value that is God Himself and the revelation that is the Scripture that cannot be broken. Truly, the psalmist said, "The wicked shall be turned into hell, and all the nations that forget God" (Psalm 9:17).

In considering this course of action we must not assume that the secular world will willingly turn en masse to the God who presides above the destinies of nations. It will take several more earthquakes, tornados, floods, and bloody battlefields to bring that to pass. God prefers not to do the work of producing repentance the hard way if He can help it.

That being the case, the initiative must lie with the church. Is there not a methodology that has not yet been tried? Indeed, there is. We need a form of evangelism, of outreach, of witness that is more than mere biblical simplicities. Christianity must articulate its case in public presentation that is characterized by theological soundness and scholarly, philosophic interpretations of life and reality. Whatever other accomplishments the church has produced in our time—and they have been many— we have not succeeded in winning the battle for the minds of men. Christianity has produced sympathy and perhaps even emotional agreement on the part of the world as it looks in the direction of the church. Still, the world has not heard us say that the God whom we serve is the only God and that one day all who live will stand before Him in judgment. Indeed, too many who profess Christ have involved themselves in sympathetic discussions with the modern pagans as to whose truth is the most applicable to the problems of life. In the process, they have neglected to announce that the Bible declares, "Let God be true, but every man a liar; as it is written, That thou mightest be justified in thy sayings, and mightest overcome when thou art judged" (Romans 3:4). The instant Christianity agrees with the pluralizers that there are many forms of truth, its cause will be lost. From that point on, Christianity will have no choice except to meander along with relativists and mumble sweet nothings about God. That meandering may appear today to be through flower-strewn pathways, but it is the funeral march to the grave.

Still, the world of modern and very confused thought is ruled by its master, John Dewey. Alas, how different it might have been.

10

New Hope for the Nations: John Maynard Keynes

"But we only owe it to ourselves!"

The world after the turn of the twentieth century was an optimistic place. The Industrial Revolution was coming on strong, promising an expanded measure of prosperity for the nations of the West. For the left, a fair degree of percolation was promised by the widening dissemination and impact of Marxist theory. For the right, the expansion of capital, with its promise of wider industrialization, seemed to be a good omen for the future. By 1910, the first airplane was flown above the beaches at Kitty Hawk. The first automobile was to belch and wheeze its way down a narrow street in one of America's cities. The railroad system had been expanded to unforeseen dimensions, reaching from coast to coast with its promise to unify a young, robust nation called America.

As we have seen, religious liberalism had taken hold in Europe and was beginning to penetrate the religious and academic worlds in the United States. It, too, brought with it a form of optimism, promising that it would deliver the culture and the churches from the narrow, legalistic views of the past and bring them into a wider, more opportune future. Behind it all, Darwin's writings—with their promise of the upward evolution of culture—were being read and believed. Even the American educational system, under the leadership of John Dewey of Columbia University, was percolating with new ideas attached to terms such as *instrumentalism* and *radical empiricism*. A sunny disposition prevailed in the first ten years of this century and brought with it a measure of happiness and a sanguine attitude about the days to come. Time-Life Books calls it the beginning of *This Fabulous Century* and gave the chapter about the first ten years of the period the title "The Cocksure Era":

> It was a splendid time, a wonderful country. Most Americans felt that way as they welcomed the twentieth century, and many of them said so, with great animation and grandiose references to peace, prosperity, and progress. From Senator Chauncey Depew of New York: "There is not a man here who does not feel four hundred percent bigger in 1900 than he did in 1896, bigger intellectually, bigger hopefully, bigger patriotically."
>
> Depew's colleague, Mark Hannah of Ohio: "Furnaces are glowing, spindles are singing their song. Happiness comes to us all with prosperity."
>
> The Reverend Newell Dwight Hillis of Brooklyn: "Laws are becoming more just, rulers humane; music is becoming sweeter and books wiser."
>
> These statements set the mood for the first decade of the new century and won for the period several titles—the Age of Optimism, the Age of Confidence, the Age of Innocence. But another tag might have seemed appropriate to an objective visitor from abroad: the Cocksure Era. For this was a time when Americans were optimistic and self-confident to an extreme; they did not merely hope for the best, they fully expected it. . . . Most people automatically assumed that all problems would be solved in the normal course of events; meanwhile, the important thing was for a man to get ahead, to earn maximum returns from bountiful opportunities.[1]

Even the prices of those days were a cause for optimism. The housewife could buy a dozen eggs for twelve cents; she could get sirloin steak for twenty-four cents a pound; and a turkey dinner cost twenty cents. The businessman had it good—

1. *This Fabulous Century: 1900-1910* (New York: Time-Life, 1969), p. 29.

taxes were minimal, and trade was moving along briskly. Many new devices were appearing on the scene, including the telephone, the typewriter, the sewing machine, the self-binding harvester. And the automobile was moving strong.

A major part of the optimism of the people of the early 1900s came from looking back at the accomplishments of the preceding century. Thirty-five years now separated Americans from their civil war, and America had become a major industrial power. Indicative of the spirit of the time were the words of Senator Albert J. Beveridge of Indiana, who said, "God has marked the American people as His chosen nation to finally lead in the regeneration of the world. This is the divine mission of America, and it holds for us all the profit, all the glory, all the happiness possible to man. We are trustees of the world's progress, guardians of its righteous peace."

By the time the twentieth century moved into its second decade, the world was still experiencing affluent times, but questions were beginning to rise. Time-Life Books says:

> For the second decade of the century was a perplexing time for Americans. These affluent times were roiled by increasing ferment and discontent. Labor unrest, rising little noticed in the previous decade, could no longer be ignored; in the first six months of 1916, the country was beset by no fewer than 2,093 strikes and lock-outs. Added to the demands of militant labor were strident voices campaigning for other causes that seemed even more radical than the six-day work week: woman suffrage, birth control, advancement for colored people, progressive education, prohibition. Most alarming of all, a million socialists were demanding the overthrow of capitalism, which—they asserted—had proved itself rotten to the core.[2]

Then, in 1914, a shot was heard: the assassination of Archduke Francis Ferdinand of Austria-Hungary at the hands of a Serbian nationalist. That assassination and many related factors led into the conflict that followed—World War I. A conservative estimate of the losses places the dead at about 10 million, along with another 20 million wounded on the battlefield. This grisly total was expanded by related starvation and epidemics in the

2. Ibid., p. 31.

years immediately after the war. Although the war was initially characterized by sprightly uniforms, colorful banners, and martial music, it became a time of carnage more frightful than the world had thought possible. It had a massive impact on national attitudes and on the thought processes by which the masses interpreted the world and their future.

For the Social Darwinists, the war was a sobering experience. After all, their philosophy implied that progress was a given, and now it appeared that anything but progress had actually occurred. Nevertheless, theirs was the hope that springs eternal, and so they joined with others in proclaiming that although human mistakes are inevitable, the evolution of society will persist in carrying us on to new heights.

For the Marxists, the war was a godsend. The socialist forces in the West used it to prove that the capitalist societies were indeed breaking down. Long had they preached that capitalism bears within itself the seeds of its own destruction. Now they could prove it. Socialist parties grew in the United States and in Europe, punctuated by colorful rallies of the workers in which they sang "The Internationale" and spoke about the inevitable socialist world revolution.

The war was a fortuitous time for the Marxists for another reason: fall of Russia to the Communists and the establishment of the first Communist dictatorship. Upon Lenin's return to Russia, he lifted his voice in fiery speeches that played upon people's disillusionment with the czar and promised them great change for the future. In their depressed circumstances, the Russian people found only the will to agree with Lenin, or at least they could not find the will to resist this man with a plan. So it was that in 1918 one of the most surprising and far-reaching revolutions in world history took place. Lenin captured Russia! At that time, the Communist party had only forty thousand followers, and with a fraction of that number they took over the broad lands of that primitive northern power, Russia. One hundred fifty million people slipped into the Communist dark age, most of them never to be heard from again. The fiery, revolutionary Lenin sensed the opportunity for Communism to move from mere ideology to control of the levers of power. That it did, to the future chagrin of the world, in those fateful days in October 1918.

To the religious liberals, the war in and of itself was of only modest consequence. Some of their strongest activity, however, came after the war, at which time they capitalized on what once again was the promise of the future. They promised, "Mankind has made its last great mistake," and set to work on capturing the religious establishment in America and England as they had done on the European continent. The liberal views of Wellhausen, with their doctrine of evolution in religion, were pressed more strongly than ever. The Roaring Twenties was the expansion of the promise of everything.

But particularly, the promise that was brought in the 1920s was economic: the promise of prosperity for everyone.

Economics became the issue.

There had been a brief depression after the war, out of which came an expansion in the economy that approached the spectacular. Everyone wanted the new products that were now moving on the market, and expansion began to move on an upward cycle. The new products produced new employment, the new employment produced the money to buy the products, and everyone was ecstatic. Mass production began to turn out radios, electric refrigerators, modern automobiles, shinier bathroom fixtures, and a thousand other things that could hardly be made fast enough to satisfy the appetite of a voracious populous.

Time-Life Books reports:

> Corporate profits were up. Thanks to new techniques of mass production, many manufacturers netted huge sums that they liberally plowed back into plant expansion. In 1923, U. S. Steel was operating so efficiently that it was able to reduce its work day from twelve to eight hours, to employ seventeen thousand additional workers, to raise wages, and yet, amazingly, to show an increase in profits.
>
> Income was up in most lines of endeavor. Even the industrial workers, whose strikes for higher pay had availed them little in the previous decade, benefitted from company largesse and enjoyed a higher standard of living. To round out the happy picture, prices were stable, savings and life insurance doubled; and business was given an added impetus by the growth of chain stores

and installment buying. With all these factors reenforcing the upward spiral, prosperity seemed to have no ceiling.[3]

This spiral of economic activity and prosperity created company profits in such spectacular amounts that new attention was paid by everyone to the rising values in the stock market. By 1928, the prices of stocks had soared to an unbelievable level. Tens of thousands of ordinary people across the nation moved into the stock market in the hopes of making an instant killing. A valet of one of the brokers made $250,000, and a nurse made $30,000; this miracle financing occurred in very short order.

Optimism turned to euphoria, and euphoria to ecstasy. More people than ever began to dream about riches, to the point where one and a half million Americans became involved in the market. They came bringing their dreams with them, confident that the amazing rise of stock prices would be the escalator that would take them to a level of possessions beyond their wildest dreams. Anyone in those days who lifted a word of warning was thought a Cassandra. Yes, those with warnings were more than pessimistic—they were positively unpatriotic.

A related development of those days was the unprecedented expansion of installment buying—purchasing goods by making payments over time. Between 1920 and 1929, installment purchases quintupled and reached 6 billion dollars annually. Installment buying accounted for the purchase of 90 percent of all pianos, sewing machines, and washing machines sold. A high percentage of sales of vacuum cleaners, radios, and refrigerators were made on installment, not to speak of the purchase of furniture and automobiles.

Installment buying seemed like a miracle. How easy it was to buy nearly anything for ten dollars down and fifteen dollars a month! People ignored the fact that installment buying added between 10 and 40 percent to the cost of an article. One "unpatriotic" banker warned against installment buying, saying that it was "mortgaging future earnings for the gratification of present-

3. Ibid., p. 96.

day pleasures," but his was a voice surely unheeded. The escalator kept on rising.

An interesting gauge of the times is reported by Time-Life Books: "New-fangled economists considered credit buying a healthy handmaiden of prosperity. One such optimist, writing in *Collier's Weekly*, suggested that the phrase, 'Smith has large debts,' was not really damning, but complimentary, for it meant that 'Smith has a fine line of credit.'"[4]

Another oncoming and soon-to-be major factor of those days was the advent of the electronic media. At the time, "electronic media" meant radio, and it was the universal craze. No new product those days met with greater success than the amazing machine that could bring into your home a voice from across the nation—yes, even from around the world.

Radio had its beginning in 1920 at station KDKA in Pittsburgh, announcing the returns of the Harding-Cox presidential election. So inspiring was the response to this broadcast that KDKA scheduled regular broadcasting of news, music, and the worship services of one of the local churches. By the end of the decade, 618 radio stations were beaming forth across the nation, and networks were regularly broadcasting from coast to coast. All of this stimulated the interest in this free home entertainment, such that radio sales rose from less than $2 million in 1920 to above $600 million in 1929.

In true American fashion, radio broadcasting was accompanied by radio advertising. It was in the 1920s that those commercial enterprises that could take advantage of radio promotion saw gigantic expansion. That was because that radio promotion created such an interest in their products that nothing could stop the desire of people to respond affirmatively to the voice of advertising. The time was accurately described as "the golden dawn of total advertising." Stock prices were riding a rocket upward and ever upward; prosperity seemed certain for every man.

Then came Black Tuesday, October 29, 1929.

That was the day of the stock market crash. Between late October and mid-November of that year, stock prices lost more

4. Ibid.

than 40 percent of their total valuation—a drop of $30 billion in paper value. The collapse, of course, was traced to a number of causes. One was the fact that stocks were priced far, far above their real value, prices based on no economic justification whatsover.

In addition, stocks could be purchased for as little as a 10 percent margin, with the balance of the purchase price financed by loans from the stockbrokers. As a consequence, when the market began to fall, overextended investors were required to put up additional margin, something many of them could not do. That drove the market into an even steeper and wider descent, with brokers themselves being carried away by the cataract of financial ruin rolling upon America and the world.

Sick jokes about the market went everywhere. A common subject was the talk of suicide—but contrary to popular myth today, the actual suicide rate was higher in the few months before the crash than it was just after it.

Still, the fact remains that the crash in 1929 of the American stock market is still thought of as the most memorable day in the economic history of civilization. From that day on, anything that had anything to do with money or investments was to be more carefully watched, more judiciously handled. Never again was anything that carried the name *economics* to be thought of as automatic, ever-growing, never-failing.

It is also true that Black Tuesday stimulated the study of that nearly occultic science called economics. Understandably, everyone from the academicians to the bootblacks asked the questions: "Why? Why did it happen? How could it have been avoided? What can we do to restructure it all? Is there a tie-in between economics and politics? How shall we understand this matter of money, and what can we do to put the nation and the world back on the road to recovery?"

The pursuit of the answers to those questions became the full-time occupation of more thoughtful people than ever. Still, no answer seemed to be forthcoming, and the West moved into the gray, cheerless era called the Great Depression. Down went the statistics on employment, as the bread lines, soup kitchens, and rescue missions did a thriving business at simply keeping unemployed workers and their families alive. Few who are young today can appreciate the deep pall of despondency that settled upon a hopeless nation during the days of the Great Depression. Life was over; the bright dream of the 1920s had turned into a cruel farce. "Who is to blame?" people asked. "What shall we do about the future?" So it was that as the world moved into the 1930s, discouragement was large, hopes were small, and to promise possibilities in the future seemed like the words of a charlatan.

As the nation moved through the Great Depression, it thought deeply about what had happened and tried to analyze why it had happened. Only then did it take the time to remember that the previous message of unlimited prosperity was really a charade. Banks were actually failing before the crash at a rate of two per day. The nation angrily remembered that it was constantly the object of reassuring speeches by politicians, businessmen, economists, and other academicians, who claimed the nation was marching along a permanently high plateau with nothing to worry about. Never again was the world quite as confident in the promises of people who were supposed to know what they were talking about. One of the worst aspects of the Great Depression was that answers were not forthcoming, and it appeared that there would never be relief from the hopelessness the nation faced. The nation sang "Happy Days Are Here Again," but in 1930 the national income fell from $87 billion to $75 billion. It dropped to $59 billion in 1931, and to $42 billion in 1932.

In 1932, the nation took political vengeance on the party in power. The Republicans nominated Herbert Hoover once again, whereas the Democrats nominated a New York patrician by the name of Franklin D. Roosevelt. Hoover ran on a platform of stability and the slogan "We can make it through," while Roosevelt promised a "New Deal." As we all know, the New Deal caught the imagination of the people, and Roosevelt was elected by a landslide. The prospects under the Roosevelt administration brought new hope to the people.

By 1933, however, problems still persisted, and it seemed as if nothing would help the situation. The problem of unemployment especially dispirited the people and spread a sense of hopelessness. Heilbroner said of this period:

It was the unemployment that was hardest to bear. The jobless millions were like an embolism in the nation's vital circulation; and while their indisputable existence argued more forcibly than any text that something was wrong with the system, the economists wrung their hands and racked their brains and called upon the spirit of Adam Smith, but could offer neither diagnosis nor remedy. Unemployment—this kind of unemployment—was simply not listed among the possible ills of the system: it was absurd, impossible, unreasonable, and paradoxical. But it was there.[5]

Yes, the economic system of that day, especially the element of unemployment, was a paradox. There was a great need for further production, and yet that need existed next to millions who were vainly seeking employment. The economic system of that day was a mystery of mysteries—and no one had the formula for solving it.

Then came a man with a solution. He offered a new way of thinking about economics that was startlingly different but, when explained, seemed very plausible. Along with this, he appeared to have the personal credentials, the knowledge, and the world awareness that lent gravity to his economic views. He had already made a personal fortune in world finance and was one of Britain's most respected and *avant-garde* intellectuals. He was chairman of a life insurance company but an intellectual of the first order. He appeared on the scene with what seemed to be the only workable solution to the economic problems of that day.

His name was John Maynard Keynes.

The solution he proposed and the sense in which he continues to rule the world from the grave can be summed up in the words *Keynesian economics*. Keynesian economics changed the face of the world and affects every living person.

Who was this man, this world changer?

Keynes was a well-bred Englishman born in 1883 (the year of Karl Marx's death). In the early years of his education, Keynes demonstrated himself to be intellectually brilliant and a convincing, communicative salesman of his ideas to his schoolmates. By the age of fourteen, he had won a scholarship to Eton,

5. Robert Heilbroner, *The Worldly Philosophers* (New York: Simon & Schuster, 1986), p. 253.

probably the most sophisticated boys' school in Britain. He had great success as a student there, and then went to King's College at Cambridge. There Keynes again showed his brilliance and demonstrated himself to be a winning debater and thoroughly capable at every other form of interaction with his professors and his peers; he so impressed his professors that they asked him to consider becoming a full-time economist. But though the door was open to him to pursue an academic career, he had little money at that time and replied that he wanted instead to manage a railway or organize a trust.

Temporarily, however, he went into the civil service for the British government, passing his tests with brilliance, though, interestingly enough, his lowest mark was in the economics section.

By 1907, Keynes found himself in the India Office in the service of his government. He found the work boring and spent his rather sizable amount of spare time working on a mathematical treatise and other forms of economic research. After two years, he tired of his work in India and resigned to return to England. Despite his boredom with his involvement in the Office of Indian Affairs, he still wrote a treatise in 1913, *Indian Currency and Finance*, which many considered to be little short of a masterpiece. As a result, when he was but twenty-nine years old, he was invited to be a member of a newly formed Royal Commission on the problems of currency in India. At Cambridge he became the editor of the *Economic Journal*, Britain's most influential economic publication, holding that post for the next thirty-three years.

As World War I drew near, Keynes was called by his government to the Treasury and given the assignment of working on the overseas finances of Britain. In this position he was soon dealing in the currencies of Spain, Germany, France, Italy, the United States, and others. One in the midst of such a swirl of economic instruments could not help but develop awareness, convictions, and even theories as to what might be done with those unstable things called national currencies.

Very soon, as we may guess, he became an important figure in the Treasury. Many thought that he contributed more in his post to the winning of the war than any other person in civilian life.

In the years between the wars, Keynes gained the reputation of being an important person in the field of economics, especially economics as it relates to government. Following the war, he went to Paris as Deputy for the Chancellor of the Exchequer on the Supreme Economic Council and possessed full power to make decisions as a representative of the Treasury at the Peace Conference. Although he did not have ultimate decision-making power at the conference, he was able to observe, comment, be frustrated, and strongly propose what he would do if he were in the decision-making place. He strongly disagreed with the decisions made at the 1919 Peace Conference, saying that he had never been so miserable, and felt that the peace basis was outrageous and impossible and could never bring anything but misfortune. The reparations that Germany was required to pay in this Carthaginian peace were beyond its ability to fulfill. Keynes properly foresaw that this would merely lead to great resentment on the part of the Germans and an even stronger resurgence of German autarchy and militarism.

Despairing of any good possibilities from the conference, he resigned. He then set to writing and produced his repudiation of the conference, *The Economic Consequences of the Peace*. This polemic, written in the heat of passion, established him as a formidable economic mind. Of the conference, he wrote:

> The Council of Four paid no attention to these issues [of the resuscitation of Europe], being preoccupied with others: Clemenceau to crush the economic life of his enemy, Lloyd George to do a deal and bring home something that would pass muster for a week, the President to do nothing that was not just and right. It is an extraordinary fact that the fundamental problems of a Europe starving and disintegrating before their eyes, was the one question in which it was impossible to arouse the interest of the Four. Reparation was their main excursion into the economic field, and they settled it as a problem of theology, of politics, of electoral chicane, from every point of view except that of the economic future of the States whose destiny they were handling.[6]

6. Ibid., p. 260.

It was clear from *The Economic Consequences of the Peace* that Keynes possessed a rapier-like mind and a fascinating facility with words. The book, however, was more than verbal grandstanding but was a serious warning to the world of the tragic consequences sure to follow the ill-considered treaty. Because the treaty was manifestly unworkable even in the near term, the book was considered prescient and was an immense success. By 1924, the nations initiated the long promises of undoing the decisions of 1919, which only further confirmed Keynes as an economist.

Out of all this, Keynes became famous. So that he could become independently wealthy enough to continue to operate on the high levels of statecraft, for a time he applied his insights about economics to the task of making money. Disdaining inside information, he made a fortune on Wall Street. Especially did he speculate in international currency markets. Here experience paid off, and Keynes was able to make himself a multimillionaire. His own ability to make money, a rather rare credential for an economist, further enhanced his reputation.

Keynes then began to think more deeply about the global economy and what was needed to prevent such disasters as the Great Depression of 1929-33. Eventually he came to conclusions that were to be of profound influence on the Roosevelt administration. Keynes, through Roosevelt, became the economist most decisive in American economic thinking and thereby gained in America the influence he already had in England and on the European continent. An understanding of economic theory Keynes developed will give us a clue to Keynes's pervasive influence to this day.

The standard concept of economics at that time was that wide variations in the economy between inflation and depression were inevitable. However, the thought was that there were built into the economy on a somewhat automatic basis the factors that could pull an economy upward from depression and ease it downward from an inflationary peak. The argument was that, during periods of depression, savings would rise and therefore interest rates would fall, making money available for industrial expansion. Industry would then expand, increasing employment and causing the economy to rise, thereby producing further investment. Interest rates would then rise, reducing savings and causing a downturn in the economy. So the cycle would continue with dependable safety switches built in at the top and the bottom of the business cycle.

That was the view of the way the economic cycle worked, standard variations of which were held by the conventional economists. Keynes, however, believed that there was a flaw in the view. The theory did not work the way it should have during the Great Depression. Keynes argued that the standard view in no way guaranteed that the economy would go up again, stimulated simply by the businessman's motivation to encourage production and plant building because of lower interest rates. Keynes asserted that the missing element in the theory was the notion that at the bottom of the business cycle there would be insufficient money in savings to reduce interest rates and cause the cycle to move up again.

For Keynes, the stimulant necessary to cause an economy to move upward toward prosperity from a depression did not lie in the static values of savings and investment. He held, rather, that it was *enterprise* that caused an upward economic movement.

Moreover, Keynes argued, business investment and enterprise was not and could not be a constant and dependable thing. Expansion of a given business would reach the point where it was sufficient and where overexpansion would lead to costly investment in buildings and equipment beyond the demand for the product. The businessman, therefore, could not be expected to invest constantly, and thus there was no constant guarantee of an upward spiral in the economy.

The book that grew out of these theories was Keynes's most famous and striking book, *The General Theory of Employment, Interest, and Money*. This complicated treatise makes for demanding reading, but it actually presents but a few pointed thoughts, which Heilbroner reviews.

> First, an economy in depression could stay there. There was nothing inherent in the economic mechanism situation to pull it out. One could have "equilibrium" with unemployment, even massive unemployment.

Second, prosperity depended on investment. If business spending for capital equipment fell, a spiral of contraction would begin. Only if business investment rose would a spiral of expansion follow.

And third, investment was an undependable drive wheel for the economy. Uncertainty, not assurance, lay at the very core of capitalism. Through no fault of the businessman it was constantly threatened with satiety, satiety spelled economic shrinkage.[7]

In a word, the economy lived in the shadow of collapse.

Keynes believed that there had to be another input brought into play in the economy—a tonic, a catalyst—to get it moving again. In fact, he believed that the policies announced in the early days of the New Deal demonstrated that new factor. In this, he referred to an element proposed in the veritable flood of social legislation the Congress hoped would stimulate the economy, thereby improving the morale of a discontented nation. That tonic, which was precisely Keynes's recommendation, was specific, planned, *government investment*.

For Keynes, government investment was the golden panacea. He preached that the major responsibility of government was to create full employment even if it had to borrow money and assume mounting debt to do so. Keynes believed that America, even the entire Western world, was facing a major economic catastrophe and possible collapse. This impending collapse, he believed, had come about because of the lack of investment on the part of business, and therefore the government must take up the slack and invest in the economy.

Keynes presented this panacea in articulate, convincing fashion. The panacea was being applied in the United States, and he recommended it for other nations. It is probable that Keynes did not envision government intervention as a *permanent* factor in the economy but rather saw it as a temporary stimulant to bring on further employment and raise the levels of business investment activity. It is certain that he did not foresee that he was in fact creating a permanent condition whereby government borrowing and deficit spending would become the ex-

7. Ibid., pp. 274-75.

pected—indeed, the recommended—course of action for the nations.

He might well have taken the time to notice that the activity of the New Deal in the 1930s in America was but a short-term and costly answer to the problems of unemployment and poverty. The vast amounts of government spending in the New Deal could have been shown to be an unwise course, had it not been for the advent of a cataclysm so large as to put every economic theory on hold until it passed.

That cataclysm was World War II. In World War II, government spending rose, as if on an elevator, to $103 billion annually, a figure considered astronomical at the time. So it was that the day in which the government must pay the bill was pushed into the future by the advent of the war.

Keynes also did not foresee that the rise in government spending and intervention in the economy would be mistrusted by the business community. Questions that had to do with "the role of government in the economy" and how this new philosophy related to labor unions, government guarantees of financial institutions like the banks and the savings and loans, and a dozen other economic problems had not yet been answered. Some of these questions are being answered today, as the government faces its obligation of hundreds of billions of dollars of guarantees in failures it never foresaw.

It may well be said that the philosophy Keynes brought to the center of the world's thinking could be summed up in the maxim "The government has all the answers." Keynes thought he had proved that government intervention would move the economy; government guarantees would stabilize the banks; government protection would satisfy the labor unions; government regulation would stabilize transportation, travel, the media, housing, mortgages, pension funds, and retirement plans; and a thousand other things in which the government is now called upon to produce stability.

Keynesian economics preaches the doctrine that the government is the final resource. It can answer every problem; it can create something out of nothing, namely, prosperity. What can this mean except that the government is God?

The government is God! That is Keynesian economics.

The idea that the government can do it all was the unspoken concept behind Keynesian economics. That assumption allowed Keynes to produce immediately satisfying, short-term solutions. Someone is reported to have asked Keynes, "Yes, this appears to work in the short term, but what about the long-term consequences?" Keynes's famous answer was, "In the long term, we are all dead."

In response to the Keynesian view, many voices have been lifted that ask the questions: Where does all the money come from? From what source can we continue to borrow *ad infinitum* the money that is needed in larger and larger amounts for the government to be the nurturer and manager of everything?

The answer which came out of the Roosevelt administration in the 1930s was deceptively simple: That is no problem because, of course, *we only owe it to ourselves.*

We owe it to ourselves!

That answer, of course, was initially true. Government bonds were issued in the 1930s to finance the borrowing of the federal establishment. They were issued in the 1940s and called war bonds to finance the cost of the global conflict. Government bonds have been issued in greater and greater amounts since that time, and now it has come the point where it is impossible to disguise the fact that the federal establishment in the United States is facing a most severe economic crisis due to its staggering debt.

Once upon a time, the admission of a government deficit was a great embarrassment to the politician. Presidential candidates from both parties ran on the platform of promising to balance the budget and pay off the national debt. The claim even became a serious plank in political platforms and was sometimes actually believed by a gullible populace. But there came a time when this all changed. There was even perhaps a specific point of time at which it changed. In the middle of his administration, conservative Republican Richard Nixon made a surprising public confession. He said, "I am a Keynesian."

When we heard that statement, our hearts skipped a beat, but there it was. From that point on, no presidential candidate has seriously promised to reduce the debt, and most of them merely mumble about balancing the budget. In a kind of a desperation, the Congress passed the Gramm-Rudman Act in which it was required that the deficit be reduced each year until finally government income would more than match expenditures, and government obligation move down rather than up.

The record is now clear that even the Gramm-Rudman Act was a chimerical promise. In fact, the government has even resorted to the ploy of disguising the true amount of the deficit by expropriating the Social Security fund gained from Social Security "contributions" and applying the money to the deficit. As a consequence, the annual deficit runs nearly $100 billion larger than the stated figure.

But now a crisis looms. The staggering debt of the federal government of the United States has passed through the $3.3 trillion mark. It can be expected to continue to rise, because there is no safety factor in Keynesian economics or in any other economic theory whereby a sum so large can be digested or properly handled.

Three point three trillion dollars is a lot of money!

How long do you think it would take to count to *one trillion* if one counted at one dollar per second, twenty-four hours of every day? It would take *thirty-two thousand years.* And if one were to count the dollars of the current U.S. deficit at a rate of one dollar per second, it would take more than *one hundred thousand years.*

In addition to the obligations on the books of the federal government, there are other commitments it must meet. It must meet its promise to fund military retirement, civil service retirement, Social Security payments, and many, many obligations that do not appear as accounts payable because they have not yet come due.

What happens when they do come due? Will millions of the youth of our nation react patiently to the news that there is no money left to pay for their retirement years? Who will give an answer for the empty Treasury and the consequent jeopardy in which our future senior citizens will find themselves?

The answer is that those obligations will be met through the twin programs of a rising population and controlled inflation.

That leads to the question, Will we have a rising population? At this point arises another consideration in the economic equation—the practice of abortion that is even now taking place in American life. Americans, by deliberate malice aforethought, are killing four thousand unborn children every day in the abortion mills of this land. Consequently, twenty million doctors, attorneys, nurses, airplane pilots, government workers, wage earners, and bearers of the burden will not exist in the future of America. Then the nation will truly sing "Where Have All the Children Gone?" It will discover what it means not to have someone to listen to the stethoscopes, push the wheelchairs, or operate the machinery that will make for the comfort of the aged and the life of society. In that the official position is now "zero population growth," and in that we are accomplishing that goal through the application of the knife and saline injection, we cannot guarantee that funds will be available in the future out of current cash flow to meet the present cost of yesterday's profligacy.

Controlled inflation is a tricky business. Inflation, by its very nature, is based upon components that in days gone by have stubbornly refused to be controlled. Inflation is affected by productivity, interest rates, careful management, personal competence, lack of greed, and other factors. Few management systems, including dictatorships, have been able to control those factors.

We must also remember that the economic situation of any given nation is related to the world economy. Decisions made in Japan, in Germany, in the new and powerful European Common Market, in the diamond mines of South Africa, and around military tables in the Kremlin will be factors—uncontrollable by America—that will impact upon us and other nations. In the old days of isolationism, nations could argue that they were masters of their own destiny. That day is gone forever. The industry of a Japanese carmaker can steal the hubcaps and even the wheels off a Cadillac in Detroit. It is all tied together, and the knots are increasingly out of the reach of the planners in the American hemisphere.

It is possible to show that the Keynesian doctrine that government can do it all is false in the short term and false in the long term. The days of stable economies in Western nations were the days in which the government served as an umpire, not as a member, of one or another of the teams. The government called the balls and strikes, but the competent entrepreneurs and capable workers produced the results. Now, under its mandate to be God, the government tilts the playing field, juggles the score, and fixes the game before the last batter has appeared. By doing so, it produces a game that cannot be fairly won even by the most worthy.

It could be argued that the government has the right to do all this, if it could at the same time be proved that the government is controlled by the most brilliant, the most moral, the most competent of men. Were the capitals in our world inhabited by tall men, sun-crowned, who live above the fog in public duty and in private thinking, then we might take courage. But, alas, we look through our tears at the dreadful activities of small men who have been accidentally escalated to positions of undeserved power, to positions above the level of their competence. How else can we explain staggering debt, huge deficits, lost wars, and costly scandals? Any government that expands its control, while at the same time reducing its competence to exercise that control, will soon begin to sense the hitherto solid ground quivering beneath its feet.

The Keynesian view that the government can do it all while solving every one of its problems will soon be put to the ultimate test. That test is survival. The Congress of the United States, the parliaments, and the leadership groups of virtually every nation on earth are now meeting under the shadow of mounting economic crisis. Each one has proved that it is totally unable to reduce its spending. Therefore, the question will center on new sources of revenue and how an already beleaguered people can have more money extracted from them. This unhappy scenario is being repeated across the world today because government after government has taken to itself a myriad of obligations it cannot and will not fulfill. In the economy of God, the government has never been appointed to be the father, the mother, the rich uncle, the provider, or the savior of each one of its individual people. When the government begins to play God, it will find itself increasingly satanic in its activity and in its reputation.

There remains a question, one to which John Maynard Keynes was inattentive: Where will the money come from? In the 1930s and 1940s it was sufficient for the nation to say, "It doesn't matter, we only owe it to ourselves!" But now, this mythical committee called "ourselves" is ceasing to exist as a viable economic entity. That committee called "ourselves" is now Japanese, German, Dutch, and British and may soon be joined by many others. The money we must borrow today comes from far away.

In order to make this borrowing possible it has become imperative for the industrial nations of the world to set up an international economic construct. There must be a world bank, a set of multinational commissions, and other financial cartels that are a part of a mounting and necessary construct called international finance. We do not now have the remaining money to borrow from ourselves, and so we must turn to the international financial markets. But, alas, it is a finite world. How long will this stream of available international finance continue to flow? How long will the interest rates be manageable? How long will former enemies on many a battlefield continue to be our present friends? When will they decide that it is time to overturn the international financial and political structure of earth? Soon the answers to those questions will be entirely up to them, because they are the pipers and we are the dancers, the payees.

Keynes has succeeded in putting the nations of the world in the position where they must come together under a new form of international control. The final, stark necessity toward which all of the world is heading is an international economic community, an international management committee—yes, a world government. Foreseeing this, Europe is already pulling itself together to become the most powerful economic cartel in the world. Seeing this, Japan is gathering the nations of the Pacific rim to produce the economic unity crucial to their survival. Japan, the net creditor nation of the world, can do this with ease.

The United States is the net debtor nation of the world. It is not evident how easily it can gather the remaining nations of the world into an international cartel. Keynes may well have planted the time bomb of economic catastrophe set to explode on the North American continent. When that time bomb explodes, will he be here with a new theory to help us? Indeed not, for he watches from his grave. His exasperating insistence that the government is God continues with us. Astonishingly, the Keynesian view continues to have avid followers. They buy this infernal package in the short run. They seem not to have heard that "in the long run we are all dead."

A final question is in order: Is Keynes really to be blamed for all of this? We think not. Keynes, along with the others who rule from their graves, can only exercise power because he panders to the irascible nature of mankind. Keynesian economics gave to the Roosevelt administration and to successive governments of this and other lands an excuse to live the lives of economic dissipation, which was their intention in the first place.

The resolute man or woman is not easily persuaded to become a humble supplicant for government support. Being responsible, which is man's highest function, the strong human being does not concede to the proposition that the government owns, operates, and deserves it all. He lives and moves and has his being in a source other than the halls of a congress or parliament. He is a son of the living God. He is therefore confident that true riches are not the coins of the realm and that true government is the kingdom of heaven, which, despite temporary evidence to the contrary, rules over all. No, Keynes was but the catalyst whereby the incompetent majorities could subdue the competent minorities and use the government as a club to bring it to pass. Sensing the hopelessness of the course that has been produced by Keynesian economics, we rejoice that the course of any individual can still be the pursuit of the will of the One whose kingdom is not of this world.

11

The Advent of Diffusion: Søren Kierkegaard

"I conceived it as my task to create difficulties everywhere."

The man who spoke those words produced in the world a wide result that is measurable and yet mysterious. Born in 1813 and dying in 1855, he said what he said, lived as he lived, and wrote what he wrote before the time of most of the other historical provocateurs who are the object of our attention. The others knew little about him; and if they did know, cared even less. Nevertheless, he built a secret tunnel under their lives and years that was to surface and bring his ideas to the fore long after they were gone. The writings of this man were sometimes clear, but more often they were frustratingly cryptic. An interesting fact about the products of his facile pen is that they needed to wait one hundred slumbering and inattentive years before they were even translated into the English language. When they appeared in English, they made a stunning impact, for they were just the ideas for which the world was waiting.

Who was this man?

He was called "the melancholy Dane," but sometimes that melancholy gave way to what can only be called "divine intoxication."

His name is Søren Kierkegaard.

This remarkable man was one of the most prodigious writers of his day. Considering the content of his paragraphs and the whiplash nature of his presentations, we find ourselves at least mildly surprised that he was the object of nearly no attention in the English-speaking world until almost one hundred years after the expiration of his short but thoughtful life. A possible explanation of this hiatus in his public reputation may be accounted for by the makeup of Western society during the period in which he wrote.

In the area of religion and its related philosophic views, this century has been as colorful as any and more than most. On the religious side, the impact of Wellhausen's denial of the true inspiration of the Bible and the consequent rise of religious liberalism came sweeping into the West at about the turn of the century. The brand of religion contemplated at that time, if religion was considered at all, was liberal Christianity. From about 1910 through the 1940s, the liberal view was the prevalent mode of thinking in the great denominations, the large seminaries and colleges of the East, and, to a great extent, among the general public. Therefore, groundless human optimism replaced year by year the categoric theological tenets that are taught in the Bible. As the Bible became more and more a human book, it became more and more irrelevant. As the true deity of Jesus Christ was denied, He became merely an interesting teacher and finally almost an imposter who brought discomfort to the natural man in his complacency. The cross, to the liberals, became more and more an embarrassment and less and less explicable. Finally, the death of Christ was virtually denied as a historical fact and became a mythological paradigm for noble sacrifice a man might be called upon to express through the way he lived.

The need for personal salvation slipped away as education, optimism, positive thinking, good works, and noble ideals became its substitute. In some circles, salvation ceased to mean everlasting life but instead came to mean deliverance from meanness and selfishness, a concept in perfect harmony with the increasingly popular notion of Darwinian evolution. In liberalism, the object of a Christian's hope for the future was shifted from the return of Christ to a hope, and then a certainty, of improving the world. Any idea of Christ's returning to quell evil in a violent battle and then to reign with a rod of iron was thought absurd. For the liberal, the hope of the future was the church's success in its ever-growing mission to improve humanity. If Christ were to return at all, the mission of the church was to so uplift society as to make it a fit place to which the Messiah might without embarrassment return.

Through the '20s and '30s, the liberal view moved from optimism to the near-declaration of a human millennium soon to come. As a custodian of the needed management for the future, the conciliar movements formed the World Council of Churches, the National Council of Churches in America, and similar counterparts in other nations of the West. There is no doubt that the spirit of this amorphous thing that went under the name of Christianity was that of joyous, albeit slightly nervous, anticipation of a future that simply had to get better and better.

After all, the liberals thought, the world had now reached a level of intelligence so high it would never again see its component nations locked in the deadly embrace of war. World War I was the great lesson. Surely now mankind would reel backwards in horror at the prospect of another massive human conflict and the ghastly results that attended such an event. Even the peace movements of that day took the form of celebrations of mankind's new and irenic spirit, which was seen as the sure promise of a millennium of peace now coming as surely as the sun rises in the morning.

It was also argued, even by the religionists, that the financial crash of 1929 carried with it a blessed spiritual lesson. It taught that the people of the world should not lay up treasures that really belonged to the poor nor speculate with their hard-earned money to gain riches apart from responsible labor and valuable contributions to society. The Depression, as well, had reminded thoughtful people everywhere of the need for compassion, sharing, and charitable activity. Thus even financial reverses produced the salutary consequence of people becoming nicer and more caring toward their fellow man.

It was also argued that advances in science, technology, global communication, and related technologies now bursting upon the world would automatically produce comity between nations. During the '30s there was a strong emphasis on global awareness, and there reemerged the concept of one world brought together by the sinews of human brotherhood and understanding. The promise of the future was exhilarating indeed.

But at the same time, clouds the size of a man's hand had begun to appear in various places. The world began to hear reports of a colorful power-seeker on the continent of Europe, who promised a utopia for the people of Germany and the world they would soon have opportunity to rule. Thinking these claims to be merely the ravings of another fanatic, the world looked on with fascination and even amusement at the rise of Hitler and the advent of Nazism, which quickly took control of one of the most important nations in the world.

Germany was exactly that. It led the world in philosophy, theology, medicine, and many forms of technology, including early work on a mysterious process called *splitting the atom*. As the 1930s drew to their close, Hitler, with his thousands of brown-shirted cohorts and millions of loyal troops, was moving once again into the deadly business of war.

From Russia, as well, came enormously disquieting reports. A tyrant by the name of Joseph Stalin, it was rumored, had initiated programs of virtual extermination of the Kulaks and the Ukrainians, and had initiated severe persecutions against the Jews and the Christians of that Communist land. In those days, the world refused to believe the oft-stated intention of the Bolsheviks of bringing their revolution to the entire world. With similar credulity, the nations of the West allowed Communist party organizations to be developed in their own political structures, which allowance they were later to regret.

Something called *fascism* was also developing in Italy with a strutting dictator, Benito Mussolini. Fascism, Nazism, and Communism sounded in the mouths of their respective polemicists like very different things. As it turned out, they were merely different names for the same political excuse used by a dictator to grab a country, throttle it into submission, kill everybody who disagreed with him, and then smilingly inform the world that nothing had happened. One wonders at the penchant of Western intellectuals to debate epistemological niceties when in fact they are dealing with cruel brutalities that veil their activities with a mesh of emotional, challenging words that are without meaning.

All of this led to World War II. The thing that never could happen again was in fact happening, but in a greater, wider, and more deadly fashion than World War I. Millions of troops marched into the cauldron of flame and death, airplanes filled the skies, artillery laced the landscape, and rockets flew across the Channel and then across continents.

The massive explosion of cordite and hatred which was World War II was brought to a halt by the greatest explosion of them all. Hiroshima and Nagasaki disappeared in atomic clouds. The world, stricken dumb by these fearful onslaughts and the nuclear conclusion of it all, reeled in incomprehension, wondering as it does to this day what really happened. Forty million, perhaps fifty million had died. Trillions of dollars' worth of the world's substance had vanished into the consuming flames.

The result was that mankind was wondering anew about history, fate, destiny, and the purposes of the God above it all. They wondered how highly evolved, intelligent, compassionate, and well-intentioned human beings could ever allow such a catastrophe to happen. It was somewhat an ultimate question that was asked in those days: What shall I believe about it all? The world community turned to the church for an explanation.

But the church was not there.

The credibility of liberalism had disappeared in the bloody contest that had just ceased. Yes, the great denominations still gathered people in their churches, but the message to which they had committed their organizational existence was empty and false. So great was this the case that people by the millions felt that they had been betrayed by their religious leaders. They had listened a thousand times to the promise that the world was getting better and better, that days of peace had come, and that a human millennium was upon them. Now, when parents stood in tears by the graves of their fallen sons, they understandably wondered at the promises they had heard of an ever-improving world.

From the liberal establishment came a few mumbled apologies, but that was about it. A few older, sturdy dreamers like E. Stanley Jones traveled among the churches speaking about the need for religious unity, a global ecumenical movement, and a new start toward improving the world. Their speeches had a noxious similarity to those made after World War I, and they were received with disinterest and even resentment by those who felt that they had been betrayed by the earlier promise of a transformed world.

The result was that classic religious liberalism died.

The liberal establishment, not willing to return to the Bible as the Word of God, went looking for a new message, a new theology, a new personage whose ideas could replace a defunct and bankrupt liberalism.

The same questing was pursued also by the world of academia and even the world of primary and secondary education. The philosophies of the past seemed insufficient to persons in those arenas; as for those in the church, the theology of the past had been torn to shreds by undeniable reality. Liberalism was a myth that had been dragooned into an alley and mugged by stubborn facts. What to do? was the question. In what shall we now believe?

Into this vacuum stepped Søren Kierkegaard.

This was the time in which the writings of the melancholy Dane were discovered by the English-speaking world and examined with fascination by leaders in religion and philosophy. Kierkegaard wrote many things that are hard to understand to this very day, but it can safely be said that he gave a set of influences that changed the way in which reality is understood and redefined concepts ranging from faith to rationality.

He gave the world what philosophers call *existentialism*. He gave the church what theologians call *neoorthodoxy*. It is as though this man and his views emerged from an unseen direction and gained a foothold in the minds of men so quickly they had no opportunity to resist. His beguiling speculations about philosophy and religion immediately produced a new intellectual percolation and (which is sometimes even more interesting) a new set of fascinating table-talk subjects for the thinkers and the pseudo-intellectuals of the world. Neoorthodoxy, which few theologians understood, became the new set of assumptions behind much preaching. Existentialism, which no one understood, became a way to understand or misunderstand life. Indeed, it did not really matter which.

Søren Kierkegaard, the man who is normally known as the father of existentialism (although he and many others would deny it), was an interesting person. He was born in Copenhagen, Denmark, in 1813, and lived a relatively short and uneventful life, dying in 1855. Uneventful is certainly the word for his outward life, but all who read Kierkegaard must be convinced that inwardly he was frequently at odds with himself, stormy, frus trated, unfulfilled, and melancholy. These conflicting emotions did not come from a problematic background. His father was a wealthy merchant in Denmark and finally left his son Søren an estate large enough so that he would never have needed to work. In fact, he never did.

Kierkegaard spent most of his time in Denmark, except for short trips to Germany, and he spent a high percentage of that time in animated conversation with his friends in the coffee shops of Copenhagen. He often talked about the possibility of becoming a teacher or preacher, but he never did involve himself in either of those professions.

Instead, he wrote at great length on many subjects. It is through his writings, which compose many books, that the impact of his life is felt. In his personal interactions, he was not outgoing and greatly preferred solitude to being in a company of great numbers of people. He thought crowds were evil but still professed to enjoy the esteem and flattery which they had to offer to him once he had become a locally famous author. It took one hundred years for him to become internationally famous.

The noteworthy external events in Kierkegaard's life were few. In 1840, on September 8, he proposed to Regine Olsen, which proposal she accepted two days later. The story of that romance appears to suggest a constant equivocation in the mind of this young man. Finally, there came a complete rupture, the engagement was broken in October of 1841, and the day after the event Kierkegaard left Copenhagen for the first of three trips to Berlin. In 1841, he took the Master of Arts, at which time he presented his dissertation, *The Concept of Irony, with Constant Reference to Socrates.*

In 1834, he seriously gave himself to writing, and for the next ten years books poured from his pen in an uncontrolled torrent. He wrote no less than six books in the first year of that intense period. The response those books provoked was a stimulant to continued writing. And what writing it was! Kierkegaard is at the same time exhilarating and depressing. His writing is on the one hand a call to clarity and on the other a source of confusion. It is doubtful that anyone perfectly understands Kierkegaard, and certainly if someone told Kierkegaard he did, the melancholy Dane would announce that the speaker had not understood him at all.

Kierkegaard's translators, for example, have noted that when his cryptic *Either/Or* was published it produced a great sensation in Copenhagen, although no one was capable of understanding its subtle purpose and thus no one could adequately review it. Although Kierkegaard was the author of this work, he wrote it under a pen name, Victor Eremita, and listed that person as the editor rather than the author. In fact, the number of pen names under which Kierkegaard wrote are so numerous one wonders if the material was not deliberately intended to confuse rather than to clarify. The suspicion that the intent is confusion is to a great extent confirmed when one gets into Kierkegaard's writings themselves.

Something of Kierkegaard's ruminations can be detected in this passage from *On His Mission:*

> I was seated as usual, out of doors at the cafe in the Frederiksberg garden. . . . I had been a student for a half a score of years. Although never lazy, all my activity nevertheless was like a glittering inactivity, a kind of occupation for which I still have a great partiality, and for which perhaps I even have a little genius. I read much, spent the remainder of the day idling and thinking, or thinking and idling, but that was all it came to. . . .
>
> So there I sat and smoked my cigar until I lapsed into thought. Among other thoughts I remember these: "You are going on," I said to myself, "to become an old man, without being anything, and without really undertaking to do anything. On the other hand, wherever you look about you, in literature and in life, you see the celebrated names and figures, the precious and much

heralded men who are coming into prominence and are much talked about, the many benefactors of the age who know how to benefit mankind by making life easier and easier, some by railroads, others by omnibuses and steamboats, others by the telegraph, others by easily apprehended compendiums and short recitals of everything worth knowing, and finally the true benefactors of the age who make spiritual existence and virtue of thought easier and easier, yet more and more significant. And what are you doing?" Here my soliloquy was interrupted, for my cigar was smoked out and a new one had to be lit. So I smoked again, and then suddenly this thought flashed through my mind: "You must do something, but inasmuch as with your limited capacities it will be impossible to make anything easier than it has become, you must, with the same humanitarian enthusiasm as the others, undertake to make something harder." This notion pleased me immensely, and at the same time it flattered me to think that I, like the rest of them, would be loved and esteemed by the whole community. For when all combine in every way to make everything easier, there remains only one possible danger, namely, that the ease becomes so great that it becomes altogether too great; then there is only one want left, though it is not yet a felt want, when people will want difficulty. Out of love for mankind, and out of despair at my embarrassing situation, seeing that I had accomplished nothing and was unable to make anything easier than it had already been, and moved by a genuine interest in those who make everything easy, I conceived it as my task to create difficulties everywhere.[1]

One only needs to move through the writings of Kierkegaard to see the extent to which he fulfilled this ambition to create difficulties everywhere.

We must note that the difference between Kierkegaard and the other world changers under consideration in this book is that Kierkegaard was a Christian. He confessed to have had a transforming religious experience as a teenager. One could wish, by the way, that in giving this testimony he would have clearly said, "I believe in the finished work of Jesus Christ on Calvary's cross, that He the God man died for my sins. I accept Him and His gift of life everlasting."

1. Walter A. Kaufmann, ed., *Existentialism from Dostoevsky to Sartre* (New York: New American Library, 1956), pp. 86-87.

However, it is reassuring to keep his Christianity in mind when he makes such statements as:

> Melancholy, incurably melancholy as I was, suffering prodigious griefs in my inmost soul, having broken in desperation from the world and all that is of the world, strictly brought up from my very childhood in the apprehension that truth must suffer and be mocked and derided, spending a definite time every day in prayers and devout meditation, and being myself personally a penitent—in short, being what I was, I found (I do not deny it) a certain sort of satisfaction in this life, in this inverse deception, a satisfaction in observing that the deception succeeded so extraordinarily, that the public and I were on the most confidential terms, that I was quite in the fashion as the preacher of a gospel of worldliness, that though I was not in possession of the sort of distinction which can only be earned by an entirely different mode of life, yet in secret (and hence the more heartily loved) I was the darling of the public, regarded by everyone as prodigiously interesting and witty. This satisfaction, which was my secret and which sometimes put me into an ecstasy, might have been a dangerous temptation.[2]

Kierkegaard spoke about melancholy and ecstasy and leaves us with that attendant touch of confusion as we read.

One might touch on the essence of Kierkegaard (although this is a dangerous presumption) by suggesting that his reputation is built around a concept summed up in the title of one of his works, *Truth Is Subjectivity*. In this presentation, Kierkegaard spoke informatively of the difference between the subjective and the objective. He said, "The objective problem consists of an inquiry into the truth of Christianity. The subjective problem concerns the relationship of the individual to Christianity."[3]

Doubtless, the Christian examiner will find this statement to be perfectly acceptable. However, Kierkegaard did some of his most exciting writing when he came down strongly on the side of subjectivity. He announced in many ways that the problem with Christianity is not that the Christian lacks knowledge but rather that he lacks passion. That, too, may be an acceptable con-

2. Ibid, p. 93.
3. Ibid., p. 112.

clusion, but many of Kierkegaard's interpreters suggest that he seems to be saying that passion is everything.

What was the effect on society of Kierkegaard's theological and philosophical concepts? The best word for that effect is the word *diffusion*. Kierkegaard appeared to take many contradictory points of view. He almost sounded like an agnostic when he denounced the State Church of Denmark and inveighed against religious establishments in general. For Kierkegaard totally believed in the individual and hated even the concept of "the group." "The crowd is the untruth," he said again and again. He inveighed most convincingly against the crowd, inointing that only the individual has significance. Kierkegaard also attacked the traditions of theology, ethics, and metaphysics, saying that they were all self-deceptions.

Kaufmann said: "He was a man in revolt, and even if one quite agrees that a revolt was called for, one may yet regret that he went much too far and that his followers have not seen fit to redress his excesses. Instead of offering a circumspect critique of reason, indicating what it can and cannot do, he tried a grand assault. . . . Kierkegaard rashly renounced clear and distinct thinking altogether."[4]

There is no doubt that Kierkegaard confirmed and denied many of the same things. On one page, he seems to contradict what he has said on the preceding page. One reads Kierkegaard with compelling interest, but the frustrations of attempting to understand him go on and on.

The result of Kierkegaard's emergence in the middle of the the twentieth century can be described as theological and philosophical diffusion. Thinking moved from the rational to the irrational; reason gave way to feeling. Final truth slipped away, and the thinking of the world became a set of self-contradictions. Theological and philosophic diffusion—that is existentialism.

Kaufmann, who wrote convincingly on this subject, gave us perhaps a more elaborate definition of existentialism, but even the use of the word *definition* defies existential philosophy. Kaufmann said:

4. Ibid., p. 17.

Existentialism is not a philosophy, but a label for several widely different revolts against traditional philosophy. Most of the living "existentialists" have repudiated this label, and a bewildered outsider might well conclude that the only thing they have in common is a marked aversion to each other. To add to the confusion, many writers of the past have frequently been hailed as members of this movement, and it is extremely doubtful whether they would have appreciated the company to which they were consigned. In view of this, it might be argued that the label "existentialism" ought to be abandoned altogether.

Certainly, existentialism is not a school of thought nor reducible to any set of tenets. The three writers who appear invariably in every list of "existentialists"— Jaspers, Heidegger, and Sartre—are not in agreement on essentials. Such alleged precursors as Pascal and Kierkegaard differed from all three men by being dedicated Christians; and Pascal was a Catholic of sorts while Kierkegaard was a Protestant. If . . . Nietzsche and Dostoevsky are included in the fold, we must make room for an impassioned anti-Christian and even a more fanatical Greek-Orthodox Russian imperialist. By the time we consider adding Rilke, Kafka, and Camus, it becomes plain that one essential feature shared by all these men was their perfervid individualism.[5]

Then follows a statement which gets to the core: "The refusal to belong to any school of thought, the repudiation of the adequacy of any body of beliefs whatever, and especially of systems, and a marked dissatisfaction with traditional philosophy as superficial, academic, and remote from life—that is the heart of existentialism."[6]

The heart of existentialism—now we have it.

But of course, to the thoughtful person, *any* definition of existentialism is itself a contradiction in terms. That is because existentialism implies contradiction, anomaly, fluidity, and a rejection of any imposed and artificial sequence. Therefore, almost anything one might say about existentialism would be in one sense or another true. For the existentialist, "this moment" is the ultimate thing. It has no necessary causes, no automatic consequences. It is significant because it brings that instant of interaction with the outer world. That instant of interaction is

5. Ibid., p. 11.
6. Ibid.

verified, not by some categoric epistemology, but by the confirming emotion, the feeling.

For the atheist existentialists like Camus, Sartre, and others, existentialism is a denial of any consistent morality. Dress as you will, fornicate with whom you will, infect whom you will, wear clothes or go naked as you will, that's the thing. The only right is what is right for you, and the only wrong is that which produces pain or inconvenience for you. There is no law, no principle, no proper course of action of any kind, so go with the vibes! Whatever is your thing, do it. You have only one time around, so go for the gusto! One could go on and on with an endless collection of incoherencies and be speaking eloquent existentialese. Nothing would be true, nothing would be false, anything goes. The very book I hold in my hand, *Existentialism: From Dostoevsky to Sartre*, has in it a penciled remark by, we presume, a college student attending the university where the book was purchased: "All we are is cocaine in the wind, man! Far out, yeah, peace, love, hard drugs."

We may be sure that the writer of those words is an existentialist. One also wonders where that young hand is now buried or where that young mind is continuing to decompose into imbecility.

But there is an astonishing thing about existentialism. While composed minds would agree that it is a form of insanity, it has become the most pervasive philosophy of our time. There is virtually no philosophy department in any major university in Western civilization that is not built on an existentialist base. There are few college students among the millions on university campuses who have not been infected by the permissiveness and the poison of existentialism. This pervasive nonphilosophical point of view has become the intellectual ground of our society. It is a mental contagion raging across the land, and it will be be difficult, if not impossible, to root it out and destroy it.

Existentialism produced the raging, resentful youth culture of the 1960s. It gave us boys who looked like girls, girls who looked like boys, and transvestites who looked like both. It gave us raving homosexuals who declared their activities existentially "OK" and launched upon society a salvo of infection that continues to explode. Thousands of these gaunt specters of humanity received graduate degrees and are now the intellectual elite of our time. The flower children of the 1960s wrote the music and hired the rock bands who proceeded to set their contradictory ideas to discordant music. Along came free love, free sex, narcotics galore, the orgy, the séance, the suicide solution, and a thousand other insults to the image of God and the life of man.

This collection of godless nonsense called existentialism has certainly produced the greatest degree of moral, intellectual, and social ruin an incredulous mankind has ever seen. But, of course, existentialism is fun! It is the "in" thing. It is saying good-bye to the squares. It is rocking around the clock or gyrating across the floor to the tunes of Eastern mystical music or heavy metal rock groups.

That's why we won't soon be rid of it. Existentialism, like Darwinism or Marxism, panders to the lower nature of a degenerate mankind. It is not merely an alternative truth but is reprobation itself. One can at least say about most pagan philosophies that they give truth a new definition and have some form of intrinsic integration. They hold together by some logic, however illicit.

Existentialism is different. It is not simply another point of view but rather is a denial of all points of view. Far from redefining truth, existentialism announces that there is no truth. There is neither final truth nor intermediate truth. There is only this one moment, without causes and without consequences.

We must also recognize that since the 1960s, the counterculture has, for the most part, endured a haircut, taken a shower, put on a suit, and walked into the boardrooms of our corporations, the halls of our schools, and even into our pulpits. It is therefore more dangerous today because it travels in the guise of pseudosophistication. Nevertheless, it is still the same old epistemological nihilism, and the ends thereof are the ways of death.

But the existentialists have had an additional influence other than in the philosophic world of academia. The influence has moved also into the realm of religion, where it even now survives in a number of forms.

As we have mentioned, in the closing days of World War II classic liberalism expired, a victim of its own contradictions.

That was when Kierkegaard and the religious existentialists were discovered by the leaders and the educators of the ecumenical denominations in America, Britain, and the European continent. Out of this influence, there was born a form of Christianity to which was attached a most interesting name, *neoorthodoxy*. Neoorthodoxy—existentialism in religion—has been with us since. It had its greatest days in the twenty years following the close of World War II. The emergence of existentialism in the theological world and its subsequent flow into the churches has been an interesting phenomenon to trace. A brief word from an authoritative source, *The New Dictionary of Theology*, may be helpful in examining this phenomenon:

> Existentialism, through Heidegger, has influenced and formed existential theology, especially in the work of Barth, Bultman, and Tillich and Macquarrie. This approach stresses the existential moment in hermeneutics and preaching, in which humanity is summoned to respond to the call of God to live an authentic life. Jesus is the perfect example of an authentic existence. The nature of being, as outlined by existentialism, has led Tillich to interpret God as the "ground of our being" rather than as a being at all. This affects both theological epistemology and ontology. Existentialist philosophy asks the fundamental human questions of existence. Theology's task is to provide the answers.
>
> Other writers such as Marcel and Weil have adopted an existential approach to theology in contrast to clinically abstract theology. For them, theology is participative and incarnational, emphasizing the ontological weight of human experience. The key is dialogue and communication as an individual (the "I") with the eternal "thou." This leads us to faith and assurance.[7]

This description of existentialism is not an easy one, but it calls attention to something relevant to the discussion of the advent of neoorthodoxy.

What happened in the advent of neoorthodoxy was that disillusioned liberals felt chagrined at the failure of the pseudo-Christianity in which they believed and which they promoted throughout the world. Needing a new foundation on which to stand, they began a swing back toward orthodoxy, much like a

7. Sinclair B. Ferguson et al., *The New Dictionary of Theology* (Downers Grove, Ill.: InterVarsity, 1988), p. 244.

pendulum returning to its center point. They were, however, unwilling to return to embrace the traditional, orthodox, "fundamentalist" Christian faith, and so they halted the process short of becoming orthodox.

The emphasis they presented used many words and expressions well known and accepted by believing Christians. The trouble was that they gave these words a new meaning. Consequently many true believers were deceived into thinking that they were listening to the grand old Christian faith, whereas in reality a new form of spiritual subversion came upon them.

One prime example of this redefining of orthodox terms is the neoorthodox version of the doctrine of divine inspiration. For the believer, all Scripture is *given by inspiration* from God. The neoorthodox theologian also uses the word *inspiration*, but, alas, with the meaning stripped away. To the neoorthodox theologian inspiration is not what happens when God gives the Word, but rather what happens when the Word impacts upon the human spirit. Therefore, it is proper to say that the neoorthodox view is not that the Bible "is" the Word of God but that it "contains" the Word of God. More correctly, the Bible "becomes" the Word of God when the Scripture interacts within the questing soul. Inspiration is, therefore, an experience for a believer, rather than a definition of the provenance of Holy Scripture.

Salvation is another debated word. Before the days of the existentialists, salvation meant to be cleansed from sin by the blood of Christ and given everlasting life. It was essentially salvation from sin that came because of the work of Christ on Calvary.

The neoorthodox view has altered this. Salvation becomes basically a psychological experience with the personality of Jesus. It is a transforming relationship rather than a quickening from the dead.

More and more, the neoorthodox view of salvation has tended to incorporate words such as *wholistic* and *realization* into their doctrine of salvation. We are to think of things such as salvation "wholistically," rather than to believe that salvation is for the discrete human spirit. The emphasis is, therefore, on realization, fulfillment, and shalom in this life, rather than on reconciliation to a holy God.

When listening to neoorthodox leaders explain Christianity, one senses a perverse reluctance on their part to admit their previous bankrupt theology. Reluctance is also evident in their careful neglect of Calvary, the blood of Christ, divine forgiveness, original sin, and other great Christian themes. Salvation becomes experience-oriented, theology becomes contextual, and ultimate truth becomes contradictory. Neoorthodoxy may well be called an improvement over the old liberalism, but the compliment is gratuitous because neoorthodoxy is a far more subtle form of spiritual subversion than was ever possible in liberalism's overt denials of basic Christianity.

This is not to say that Kierkegaard is to blame for all of these developments. Nevertheless, he still retains the title "father of existentialism," which makes his views useful data in our examination of the present philosophic and religious conditions.

The best word to briefly describe those conditions is *diffusion*. Even neoorthodoxy has been diffused into the church milieu, allowing a dozen other clever theologies to flourish in the present religious scene. At one point so deteriorated had things become along the way that one so-called theologian announceed that "God is dead." So diverse has the theological scene become that almost any cause is now pressed upon the church in the name of theology. We have urban theology, black theology, liberation theology, hispanic theology, process theology, rhetorical theology, and a score of others. Many evangelical theologians note perceptively that the period of ascendancy of a given theological view grows shorter and shorter with each emergent form of what passes for theology. *Diffusion* is the word to describe all of this.

The advent of theological diffusion has not left the evangelical movement unscathed. Even now the evangelical movement echoes with discussions in which the basic questions of evangelical conviction are being reexamined. In the days following World War II, evangelicals in churches, denominations, and especially major movements across the country operated on the basis of a basic, conservative set of theological ideas. As an old century anticipates the beginning of a new millennium, evangelicals are once again in a discussion. Interestingly, even surprisingly, evangelicals are reviewing again the answers to the old questions many thought had been settled a generation ago. Alas, those questions have not stayed settled.

The questions under new review by the evangelicals deal with fundamental tenets of the faith: Why did Christ come into the world? What must I do to be saved? What is the purpose of the church on earth? What form does the kingdom of God take in the world today? A simple comment on these matters may be helpful, for the discussion is certain to be continued in the years to come.

The question of the purpose of the coming of Christ has been partially co-opted by the liberation theologians. They announce that Jesus came into the world to bring economic liberation to the oppressed masses of earth. The old, correct answer is that He came to bring the hope of eternal life, which God, who cannot lie, promised before the world began.

In answer to the question about the basis of salvation, the new suggestion seems to be a rewriting of the verse to read, "Believe on the Lord Jesus Christ and thou shalt be put on probation." The doctrine of salvation by faith alone is now under assault by new definitions of faith, imputed righteousness, works, and the like. In this discussion, there are dangers ahead.

The purpose of the church in the world is now newly defined by a group of people who call themselves Reconstructionists. Like the old-line liberals, they hold that the role of the church is to gain control in the world, improve the social structure, and prepare society for the return of Christ. Christians, they feel, should have actual dominion over the political structure.

The prospect of the kingdom of God in the world today calls for an ever-mounting discussion. "Kingdom now" theologies offer instant healing, instant wealth, instant everything if one simply recognizes and embraces the kingdom. With these and other questions newly afloat and unresolved, evangelicals join the theological diffusion which has come upon this generation.

What will be the end of it all? It may well be that a new creative provocateur in the Kierkegaard mold will step into our midst and write another *Either/Or*. This one may call it *Both/And*. The point is that diffusion tends to create confusion, and confusion within a culture creates vulnerability. Affected by that vulnerability, the world may even now be ready to accept another global voice, a new and plausible plan, a direction for the future that may be novel but which will appear to be most plausible. The Christian who reads the prophetic Word will have the proper suspicions as to who that man will be and what all-embracing, panacea-style theology he will promote. Yes, existentialism has certainly not yet run its course. There is an ominous sound in the distance toward which these things are leading us. Could that sound be the rumble of another earthquake, the rush of another flood, the roar of another gathering storm? Sooner than we think, the answer may be upon us.

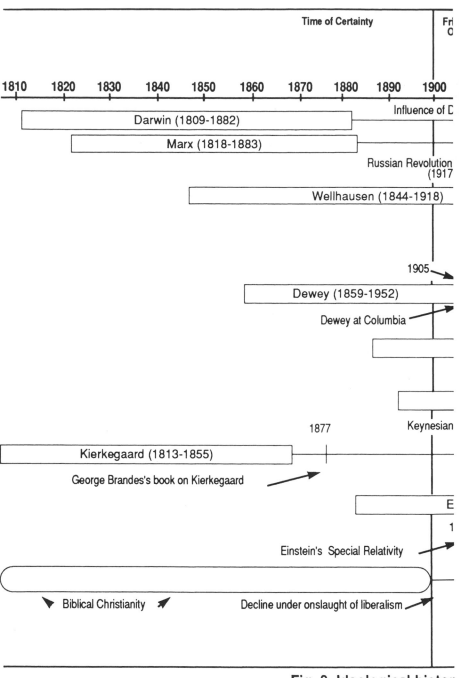

Time of Certainty

Fr
O

1810　1820　1830　1840　1850　1860　1870　1880　1890　1900

Influence of D

Darwin (1809-1882)

Marx (1818-1883)

Russian Revolution
(1917

Wellhausen (1844-1918)

1905

Dewey (1859-1952)

Dewey at Columbia

Keynesian

1877

Kierkegaard (1813-1855)

George Brandes's book on Kierkegaard

E

1

Einstein's Special Relativity

Biblical Christianity　　　　Decline under onslaught of liberalism

Fig. 8. Ideological histor

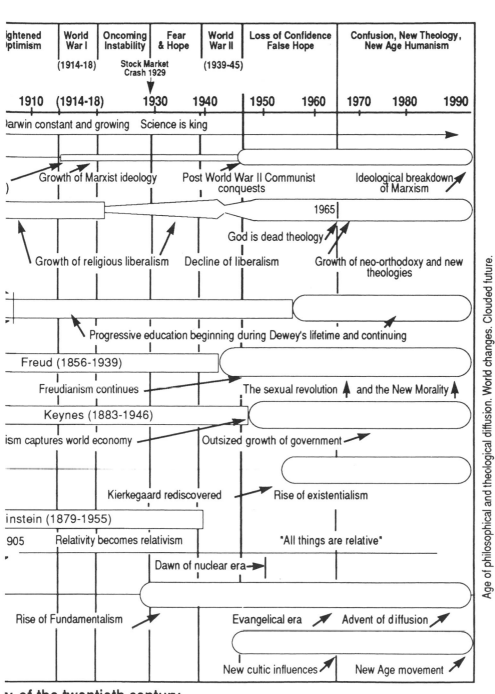

ightened ptimism	World War I	Oncoming Instability	Fear & Hope	World War II	Loss of Confidence False Hope	Confusion, New Theology, New Age Humanism
	(1914-18)	Stock Market Crash 1929		(1939-45)		

| 1910 | (1914-18) | 1930 | 1940 | 1950 | 1960 | 1970 | 1980 | 1990 |

Darwin constant and growing   Science is king

Growth of Marxist ideology   Post World War II Communist   Ideological breakdown
                                            conquests   of Marxism

1965

God is dead theology

Growth of religious liberalism   Decline of liberalism   Growth of neo-orthodoxy and new
                                                                       theologies

Progressive education beginning during Dewey's lifetime and continuing

Freud (1856-1939)

Freudianism continues ——   The sexual revolution ⬆ and the New Morality ⬆

Keynes (1883-1946)

ism captures world economy ——   Outsized growth of government ⟋

Kierkegaard rediscovered ——→ Rise of existentialism

instein (1879-1955)

905   Relativity becomes relativism   "All things are relative"

Dawn of nuclear era—⟶

Rise of Fundamentalism ⟋   Evangelical era ⟋ Advent of diffusion ⟋

New cultic influences ⟋   New Age movement ⟋

Age of philosophical and theological diffusion. World changes. Clouded future.

y of the twentieth century

12

Who Shall Overcome?

The generation that now stands at this point in history dare not move blithely onward as if, as the existentialists claim, there has been no instructive yesterday and will be no tomorrow that matters. Rather, perceptive souls of this era have the right, the responsibility, the fascinating opportunity to study the past and make a genuine attempt not to repeat its tragic elements. They must retain the joyous components from yesteryear that remain with us, if only in memory, but soberly ponder the lessons of it all. That examination of the past must not be casual, as if we were but historians filling pages for publications, but must be a serious, thoughtful examination. No one with proper sentience can read the pages of yesteryear without being reminded that the story of the past is the account of flesh and blood, contesting human wills, great purposes realized, and important causes destroyed. The colorful, fitful scenes of the past were the venues of our fathers and mothers and their parents before them. Could they speak to us now—and some do from their graves—they would certainly plead in the strongest language that the lessons they learned at the price of their fortunes and their lives be more carefully learned by us and at a cheaper price. They would surely warn us that to miss or ignore the instructive pages of the past is to be inattentive fools, fools who in our day will be consumed by the tides that might have been stopped in the days of our fathers but which today approach the all but unstoppable.

There is no question that the tides of history, surging waves of thought and action, were created by the men who now rule from their graves. By what power did they rule? Why did events occur as they did? What explanation can be given for the strange irrationalities that have swept into our time and continue to affect the course of history? What reason can we give for the impact these men made?

Those men who today rule from their graves certainly do not do so because they presented great truths, impeccable arguments, or unfalsifiable syllogisms. Rather, the first explanation for their influence is that they gave people an excuse to be what they truly are. When Lenin organized Communist cadres in the name of the philosophy of Karl Marx, who can believe that his followers fell in behind him because of a sheer love of mankind? No, indeed, for when they rose to power, they demonstrated themselves to be brutal human beings, criminal types, sadists, and murderers. They initiated an orgy of slaughter and were themselves drowned in the blood they shed, both their own and that of others.

In our time, the followers of Karl Marx have shown themselves to be selfish, hypocritical liars, amassing fortunes at the expense of the starving populous they rule. Erich Honecker of East Germany was one of those liars, with his thirty-two homes and lavish hunting preserves. Nicolae Ceausescu was another, with his immense palace.

The existentialists have done the same, pandering to the lust of people, preaching to them the doctrine of fornication without tears. These panderers to prurience are well described in the Bible: "But there were false prophets also among the people, even as there shall be false teachers among you, who secretly shall bring in destructive heresies, even denying the Lord that bought them, and bring upon themselves swift destruction. And many shall follow their pernicious ways; by reason of whom the way of truth shall be evil spoken of. And through covetousness shall they with feigned words make merchandise of you; whose judgment now for a long time lingereth not, and their destruction slumbereth not" (2 Peter 2:1-3).

The church of our time ought to take from those verses a lesson for itself. So long as large masses of people are unaffected by the transforming power of the gospel of Christ, they will be vulnerable to the perverse premises of political and religious charlatans. Should the masses in any era or in any nation fail to be reached and transformed by the message of the love of Jesus Christ and His sacrifice on the cross, these masses are tinder for a new fire ignited by the admonitions of the evil one. The Bible warns us that Satan is constantly going about seeking whom he may devour. The vulnerable ones he seeks are certainly the unevangelized, the untutored, the untransformed masses of earth. If, through the preaching of the Word, people are lifted to the place where they are partakers of the divine nature, panderers to the lower nature of man will have no fodder on which to feed. If the church fails to penetrate a society at any given time, the times subsequent to that moment of opportunity may be adverse.

A second reason for the success of the ideologists of the past is that they perceived and responded to the current forces of their history. In the days of Darwin people were looking for new layers of insulation between themselves and God. The spirit of the age was bent toward the Enlightenment, and therefore the sacred was offered on the altar of the secular.

Yes, there may be times in history during which negative forces are but inexorable, times when the night has come in which no man can work.

But that is not always the case. Sometimes negative forces have seemed so strong because believers have not been sensitive to the ebbing and flowing tides in the culture in which they are supposed to be salt and light.

Speaking about the Day of the Lord, and by implication many other special judgment days, the Scripture says: "But ye, brethren, are not in the darkness, that that day should overtake you as a thief. You are the sons of light, and the sons of the day; we are not of the night, nor of the darkness. Therefore, let us not sleep, as do others, but let us watch and be sober-minded" (1 Thessalonians 5:4-6).

Despite this admonition, too often cultural change comes upon the Christian elements of society with as great a surprise as it comes upon the people of the world. The lesson is clear: the mind of the Christian must be filled with awareness of the teaching of the Word and be perceptive as to the course of the world in which that Word is to be taught. Only then can he move strategically. The tide of history may well be bringing upon us a great and new strategic opportunity.

Let us also suggest that the success of these ideas occurred because of the absence of a timely and forceful rebuttal. On a thousand occasions in history, a foolish idea has prevailed because, figuratively speaking, no one stood up to say that the emperor had no clothes. Lenin himself, speaking of the Communist revolution in Russia, said that it could have been defeated by a hundred purposeful people in St. Petersburg who knew what they were doing. One effective debater, or even an intelligent Christian conversationalist, might have stopped Rousseau and his nonsensical arguments in one evening in the salons of Paris. By so doing, he might have prevented the French Revolution.

History teaches us that a single strong voice for God in a leaderless generation can be effective. Historians agree that the revivals of John and Charles Wesley in England did save England from the terrors of the French Revolution. Surely the single voice of Martin Luther at the Diet of Worms liberated northern Germany, then England, then major portions of the world from incarceration behind the purple curtain of Rome. Liberalism in America was impeded in some places and stopped outright in others by simple fundamentalist preachers who spoke strongly for the truth of God.

Could it be that we have forgotten the strong, amazing power of truth? Forceful speaking that presents the truth of the Word has created and will always create a great result within individuals for the perpetuation of society. For the sake of future humanity, we need to read again the telling words: "For whatsoever is born of God overcometh the world; and this is the victory that overcometh the world, even our faith. Who is he that overcometh the world, but he that believeth that Jesus is the Son of God?" (1 John 5:4-5).

Who shall overcome?

He shall overcome who believes the simple, forceful proposition, namely, that Jesus Christ is the Son of God.

Despite this promise, too many heretical speeches go unchallenged in too many denominational conventions. Too many false propositions are pressed upon young people in college chapels, even Christian college chapels. Refutation should be immediate and forceful. For want of such refutation, questing young hearts may begin to wander, never again to be retrieved for the truth.

It is clear, also, that the ideas of the seven seminal thinkers discussed in this book prevailed because of the nonexistence of overt Christian assertions on the subjects they addressed. This is not an unimportant point. Questing students in the past have often sought in vain for the Christian positions on creation, evolution, dialectical materialism, relativity, and many other subjects. But position papers are hard to come by today whereby emergent minds can be influenced early by the Christian position on the issues of our time. One dares to hope that the Christian alternative to foolish new pseudoscientific positions is being stated in the classrooms. More and more, however, the arena of contest has moved to the television networks, the radio stations, and the newspapers. Every Christian must be more articulate than ever—more thoughtful, more analytical, more ready to give a reason for the faith that is in him. Alas, one cannot help but notice that in this area we have not been well served by the theologians, who should have been responding to the contests of our time with thoughtful, biblically based answers. Keynesian economics, with its assertion that government is God, might have died aborning had there been a Christian position on government and global economics ready to meet it. The churches need once again to ask Christian theologians and intellectual leaders, "Where are you, now that we need you?"

Let us also note that the anti-Christian tides of thought prevailed in no small measure because the church had lost even its own message. Across the world Christians are often remiss, not only in not presenting position papers on global problems but also in not presenting the gospel. When the Reformation message of the gospel of the grace of God slips away from the Christian agenda, initiative, purpose, and motivation are also lost.

When we lose the gospel, we will hardly contend for the faith, because there is no remaining faith for which to contend. The church must constantly fight the dreadful slippage that can so easily take us away from the message of the cross. To us who are saved, the cross is the power of God. It must always and ever continue to be so. Dreadful consequences could come upon the eclectic evangelical movement of our time if it so pluralizes its message that no one knows which one of the twenty extant versions of the gospel is the most surely to be believed.

In thinking further about the seven men at the heart of this book, it is important to note that each was a perceptive and prolific writer. The theories they held about reality, men, nations, and the future were not babbled into the ozone. They recognized that whereas a speech lasted but for a few moments the written word produced a sustained impact. Yes, some of them were rabble-rousers, like the existential screamers at Haight-Ashbury. Still, the rabble does not stay roused apart from the progressive capturing of the mind. And that can be accomplished only by a forceful ideological message, a strong presentation of that message, and the sustained impact of the printed page.

The Communists know this especially well. They were once heard to say, "You Americans teach the people of India how to read and give them the lamps in the light of which to read. We furnish the material for them to read." That lesson ought not to be missed. The media are exciting, the kleig lights are illuminating, and the public address systems are powerful, but it is still words, those little silver bullets of logical thought, that make the sustained impact.

Dare we suggest the course of action that must be followed by the church of our time? We must have Christian thinkers who consider deeply and then write well the truth for others to read. The Christian tract, the booklet, the book, the treatise, the magazine, and the newspaper, written well and distributed wisely, are among the best instruments God has on earth to propagate His truth. The word *spoken* today will put a blip on the screen of the receptive mind, and then it will be gone. The word *written* today will print itself upon the mind behind that screen and never be forgotten.

Having considered some but perhaps not all of the reasons for the success of the ideologists of the past, we cannot avoid thinking about the future and wondering what shall unfold in the number of tomorrows available to us. In answer, let us first of all remember that the seven men we talk about in this book continue to rule from their graves. The effect of the ideas spawned and propagated by these now departed minds is an ongoing reality in our time. Boards of education continue to cast votes on questions of science, thereby pretending to prove that the majority vote establishes the truth of evolution. They have done so in the state of California, and others elsewhere will make the same infantile decisions. The existentialists continue to teach moral relativism and situation ethics. Marx continues to stride across history, even though he is limping from recent successful votes taken against him in Eastern Europe.

Could it be that the recent unexplained attitude of the Soviet Union is to be considered in another way than is suggested in the popular press? Is it possible that in releasing the Eastern European nations they are like a jet fighter dropping exhausted auxiliary tanks before it turns to do final battle with an enemy? Bear in mind that the attitude toward a totalitarian nation should be formed not by its stated intentions, which have always been deceitful, but by its real capability. In the real world, capabilities count. In the world of delusion, promises prevail. The world of delusion is neither a good nor a safe place to live.

In thinking about the future the realistic Christian will remember that alien ideologies are strong, even prevalent, throughout the world. The call, therefore, is to sobriety and vigilance. The call is also to intrepid Christian action.

In considering where we should go, we must also recognize soberly that the cause of Christ has taken severe hits in our time. Moral, financial, and sensual scandals have come upon the church like torpedoes from an alien submarine. Upon examination, it has become evident that the torpedoes have been fired and have exploded from within Christendom, their destructive force unleashed by unacceptable conduct and bad theology. Although the church must not indulge in neurotic and overly persistent self-examination, occasions come when we must examine ourselves anew. One of those occasions must be now. We may discover that the serious problem we face is not merely that some simple ones have succumbed to the lust of the flesh. We may find that we ourselves have invented too many forms of pop theology, Christian mottos, overly simple slogans, and three-word answers to everything. We may discover, for instance, that the way we have used television has trivialized the gospel, reducing our acceptance by the larger community, rather than enhancing our opportunities. We may learn that our costly, thoughtless expansions of nearly everything will bring the inevitable but impossible day in which the bill must be paid. Should we think that some of our problems are relatively minor, we may learn also from an examination of the past that some great ministries of yesterday are no more because minor problems, uncorrected, became major monsters.

But still "*Quo Vadis?*" is the question.

Great opportunities—greater than ever—are before us. Christ made the church no empty promise when He said, "Behold, I have set before thee an open door, and no man can shut it; for thou hast a little strength, and hast kept my Word, and hast not denied my name" (Revelation 3:8). That promise means that great opportunity is ours. It reminds us that opportunity does not come from cooperating circumstances, personal capability, or even the permission of some human group. Opportunity comes from Christ Himself, and it can never fail us so long as our hearts are right with Him. The church is well advised to heed the words of Daniel Burnham: "Make no little plans, they have no magic to stir man's blood and probably themselves will not be realized. Make big plans, aim high and hope and work, remembering that a noble, logical diagram, once recorded, will never die, but long after we are gone will be a living thing, asserting itself with growing intensity."

We must also remember that it is spiritually incorrect to think too much about the future without taking into account the prophetic Word. God has told us, despite the detractors of our time, that we have a more sure Word of prophecy unto which we do well to take heed as to a light that shines in a dark place. Living as we do in today's diffused scene and moving as we are into a murky future, the prophetic Word demands attention. No one can know the events of tomorrow, but the data about the future that we have in the Word of God become a light that shines through the afternoon's fading sunlight into the evening when shadows fall. We are forbidden to make concrete predictions, but we are wise to allow for the possibility that upon us have come the ends of the world.

In considering the future, we must remember that Jesus Christ the Lord presides above history and will return one day in power and great glory. That triumphant return will demonstrate for every eye to see that Christ is the Lord of history and functions precisely, perfectly, and lovingly all of the time as that efficient Lord. Then we will realize by sight, as we must now by faith, that never once in the history of mankind has an event taken place in the halls of the greatest of governments or in the remotest jungle on earth that is apart from His precise and loving permission. Remembering this—that Christ the Lord presides above history—we can think with clarity and labor with alacrity to accomplish the purpose for which we are privileged to live in this dangerous but exciting time.

We remind ourselves that the final rulership of this world and all other worlds to come is not in the hands of those who sleep under a headstone in Germany, England, France, or the United States. In the last analysis the world is ruled from the throne of the eternal God under the scepter in the right hand of Jesus Christ. Whatever may be the continuing influence of the thinkers and doers of another day, that influence will be pitiful and not to be compared with that of the sovereign God of the universe. The final chapter, which tells the account of the results of the interactions between men and nations in the narrow constrictions of time, will be as nothing when compared to the progressive and daily fulfillment of the will of the sovereign God whose universe it is.

If You Enjoyed
7 Men Who Ruled the World from the Grave,
You May Also Enjoy These Other
Quality Books from Moody Publishers:

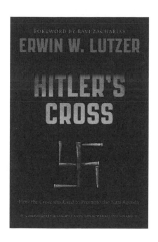

The monstrosity of Adolph Hitler's "Third Reich" remains a stunning chapter in the pages of history. Although the power by which he hypnotized the entire nation is legendary, one question in particular begs an answer.: Where was the church of Christ?

Hitler's Cross is the story of a nation whose church forgot its primary call and discovered its failure too late.

ISBN: 978-0-8024-0850-1, Paperback

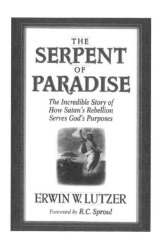

"This book is a modest attempt to put the devil in his place," says Erwin Lutzer. By pointing out that Satan cannot make a move without God's express consent.

The Serpent of Paradise will challenge popular conceptions of Satan, stimulate your faith, and lead you to worship God who does not lose— even when Satan appears to win. You will come away with a deeper understanding of Martin Luther's words, "Even the devil is God's devil."

ISBN: 978-0-8024-2720-5, Paperback